Laura Ingalls Wilder

WHO WROTE THAT?

LOUISA MAY ALCOTT

JANE AUSTEN

AVI

JUDY BLUME

BETSY BYARS

BEVERLY CLEARY

ROBERT CORMIER

BRUCE COVILLE

ROALD DAHL

CHARLES DICKENS

THEODOR GEISEL

WILL HOBBS

ANTHONY HOROWITZ

GAIL CARSON LEVINE

C.S. LEWIS

ANN M. MARTIN

L.M. MONTGOMERY

PAT MORA

SCOTT O'DELL

GARY PAULSEN

BARBARA PARK

TAMORA PIERCE

EDGAR ALLAN POE

BEATRIX POTTER

PHILIP PULLMAN

MYTHMAKER:
   THE STORY OF
   J.K. ROWLING

MAURICE SENDAK

R.L. STINE

EDWARD L.
   STRATEMEYER

E.B. WHITE

LAURA INGALLS
   WILDER

JANE YOLEN

WHO
WROTE
THAT?

Laura Ingalls Wilder

Amy Sickels

Foreword by
Kyle Zimmer

CHELSEA HOUSE
PUBLISHERS
An imprint of Infobase Publishing

Laura Ingalls Wilder

Chelsea House
An imprint of Infobase Publishing
132 West 31st Street
New York NY 10001

Library of Congress Cataloging-in-Publication Data
Sickels, Amy.
  Laura Ingalls Wilder / Amy Sickels.
    p. cm. — (Who wrote that?)
  Includes bibliographical references and index.
  ISBN-13: 978-0-7910-9525-6 (acid-free paper)
  ISBN-10: 0-7910-9525-8 (acid-free paper) 1. Wilder, Laura Ingalls, 1867-1957—
Juvenile literature. 2. Authors, American—20th century—Biography—Juvenile
literature. 3. Frontier and pioneer life—United States—Juvenile literature.
4. Children's stories—Authorship—Juvenile literature. I. Title. II. Series.
  PS3545.I342Z86 2007
  813'.52—dc22
  [B]   2007019615

Chelsea House books are available at special discounts when purchased in bulk quantities for business, associations, institutions, or sales promotions. Please call our Special Sales Department in New York at (212) 967-8800 or (800) 322-8755.

You can find Chelsea House on the World Wide Web at http://www.chelseahouse.com

Text design by Keith Trego and Erika Arroyo
Cover design by Keith Trego and Jooyoung An

Printed in the United States of America

Bang EJB 10 9 8 7 6 5 4 3 2 1

This book is printed on acid-free paper.

All links and Web addresses were checked and verified to be correct at the time of publication. Because of the dynamic nature of the Web, some addresses and links may have changed since publication and may no longer be valid.

Table of Contents

FOREWORD BY
KYLE ZIMMER
PRESIDENT, FIRST BOOK   6

1   A SMALL LOG CABIN   11

2   WESTWARD BOUND   19

3   SEEING THE WORLD TWICE   33

4   THE RAILROAD BOOM   47

5   TEACHING, MARRIAGE, AND MOTHERHOOD   57

6   THE PROMISED LAND   67

7   FROM FARMING TO WRITING   77

8   A CHILDREN'S BOOK AUTHOR IS BORN   87

9   FAME IN THE GOLDEN YEARS   97

CHRONOLOGY   109
NOTES   111
WORKS BY LAURA INGALLS WILDER   112
POPULAR BOOKS   113
POPULAR CHARACTERS   115
MAJOR AWARDS   117
BIBLIOGRAPHY   118
FURTHER READING   119
INDEX   122

FOREWORD BY
KYLE ZIMMER
PRESIDENT, FIRST BOOK

HUMANITY IS POWERED by stories. From our earliest days as thinking beings, we employed every available tool to tell each other stories. We danced, drew pictures on the walls of our caves, spoke, and sang. All of this extraordinary effort was designed to entertain, recount the news of the day, explain natural occurrences—and then gradually to build religious and cultural traditions and establish the common bonds and continuity that eventually formed civilizations. Stories are the most powerful force in the universe; they are the primary element that has distinguished our evolutionary path.

Our love of the story has not diminished with time. Enormous segments of societies are devoted to the art of storytelling. Book sales in the United States alone topped $26 billion last year; movie studios spend fortunes to create and promote stories; and the news industry is more pervasive in its presence than ever before.

There is no mystery to our fascination. Great stories are magic. They can introduce us to new cultures or remind us of the nobility and failures of our own; inspire us to greatness or scare us to death; but above all, stories provide human insight on a level that is unavailable through any other source. In fact, stories connect each of us to the rest of humanity not just in our own time, but also throughout history.

This special magic of books is the greatest treasure that we can hand down from generation to generation. In fact, that spark in a child that comes from books became the motivation for the creation of my organization, First Book, a national literacy program with a simple mission: to provide new books to the most disadvantaged children. First Book has been at work in hundreds of communities for over a decade. Every year, children in need receive millions of books through our organization, and millions more are provided through dedicated literacy institutions across the United States and around the world. In addition, groups of people dedicate themselves tirelessly to working with children to share reading and stories in every imaginable setting from schools to the streets. Of course, this Herculean effort serves many important goals. Literacy translates to productivity and employability in life and many other valid and even essential elements. But at the heart of this movement are people who love stories, love to read, and want desperately to ensure that no one misses the wonderful possibilities that reading provides.

When thinking about the importance of books, there is an overwhelming urge to cite the literary devotion of great minds. Some have written of the magnitude of the importance of literature. Amy Lowell, an American poet, captured the concept when she said, "Books are more than books. They are the life, the very heart and core of ages past, the reason why men lived and worked and died, the essence and quintessence of their lives." Others have spoken of their personal obsession with books, as in Thomas Jefferson's simple statement: "I live for books." But more compelling, perhaps, is the almost instinctive excitement in children for books and stories.

Throughout my years at First Book, I have heard truly extraordinary stories about the power of books in the lives of children. In one case, a homeless child, who had been bounced from one location to another, later resurfaced—and the only possession that he had fought to keep was the book he was given as part of a First Book distribution months earlier. More recently, I met a child who, upon receiving the book he wanted, flashed a big smile and said, "This is my big chance!" These snapshots reveal the true power of books and stories to give hope and change lives.

As these children grow up and continue to develop their love of reading, they will owe a profound debt to those volunteers who reached out to them—a debt that they may repay by reaching out to spark the next generation of readers. But there is a greater debt owed by all of us—a debt to the storytellers, the authors, who have bound us together, inspired our leaders, fueled our civilizations, and helped us put our children to sleep with their heads full of images and ideas.

WHO WROTE THAT? is a series of books dedicated to introducing us to a few of these incredible individuals. While we have almost always honored stories, we have not uniformly honored storytellers. In fact, some of the most important authors have toiled in complete obscurity throughout their lives or have been openly persecuted for the uncomfortable truths that they have laid before us. When confronted with the magnitude of their written work, we can forget that writers are people. They struggle through the same daily indignities and dental appointments, and they experience the intense joy and bottomless despair that many of us do. Yet, somehow they rise above it all to weave a powerful thread that connects us all. It is a rare honor to have the opportunity that these books provide to share the lives of these extraordinary people. Enjoy.

Laura Ingalls (far right) is shown here around the age of 12, with two of her sisters, Carrie (left) and Mary (center). Laura's books about her childhood featured Carrie and Mary prominently.

1

A Small Log Cabin

ON A COLD winter day in 1867, a baby girl was born in a small log cabin on the edge of the Big Woods in Wisconsin, just a few miles from the Mississippi River. Who could have imagined that one day, more than 60 years later, this baby girl would become a world-famous writer? Now, children and adults all over the world are familiar with the lives of the pioneer family in which that baby girl grew up.

Laura, Ma, Pa, Mary, Carrie, and Grace were all members of the Ingalls family; now, they are characters who have delighted millions of readers since the 1930s. Although the

Little House books are set during the time of the American frontier, the stories and characters continue to entertain readers in the twenty-first century. Children and young adult readers are drawn to the simple style and the vivid descriptions of the pioneer days, which are so different from our world filled with e-mails, DVDs, and video games. Many adults who read the books as children return to them, either to read them to their own children and grandchildren, or to experience the stories again themselves.

In 1932, when the first book in the series was published, Wilder had no idea that the treasured tales of her childhood would become so popular. It is hard to believe that even though the author was born more than 130 years ago, her books continue to delight children around the world.

Laura Elizabeth Ingalls was born on February 7, 1867, just two years after the Civil War ended. As the second child of Charles and Caroline Ingalls, she was two years younger than Mary, her blond-haired, blue-eyed sister. The daughters of pioneer parents, Mary and Laura lived in a snug log cabin in the Wisconsin wilderness, but they would soon pack up their belongings and journey by covered wagon to a new part of the American West.

Life was not easy in pioneer days, and people had to be self-sufficient. It was necessary to plow the fields, grow crops, hunt for food, and fight off wild animals and illnesses. Pioneers suffered through harsh winters and rainless summers. From sunrise until sunset, each person, even the young children, spent most of the day doing physical work. There were no cars or televisions or air conditioners. Can you imagine how hard this way of life must have been, without any of today's modern conveniences? It was a grueling experience.

As Wilder shows us in her Little House series, people still found ways to entertain themselves: They played music, read books, and danced together. Part of the charm

Did you know...

The success of the original Little House books has inspired many spin-off series about Laura and her family. Among them are the Little House Chapter Books and My First Little House Books, which present the stories in a simpler form for younger readers. There are also four series of books that are about the five generations of Laura Ingalls Wilder's family. The Martha Years and Charlotte Years series, written by Melissa Wiley, are fictionalized stories of Laura's great-grandmother and grandmother. The Caroline Years series, by Maria D. Wilkes and Celia Wilkins, is about Laura's mother's childhood. The Rose Years series, written by Rose's adopted grandson, Roger MacBride, follows Rose Wilder Lane from childhood to early adulthood. Children's author Cynthia Rylant wrote the book *Old Town in the Green Groves*, which covers the two years in Laura's life between *On the Banks of Plum Creek* and *By the Shores of Silver Lake*.

of the Little House books is that Wilder describes the reality of the pioneer experience in a lively and uplifting voice. The Ingalls family is happy and good natured, and although they experience many dangers and hardships, they never give up hope.

There was nothing about Wilder's childhood to suggest that she would one day become a world-famous children's book author. She spent her childhood helping with chores, attending school, and playing with her sisters. When she was older, she taught school; then she married Almanzo Wilder and had a daughter, Rose. For most of Wilder's adult life, she helped Almanzo on the farm in the Ozarks of Missouri, the place they called home. Her life revolved around her husband, her child, and the farm. Later in her life, Wilder wrote columns for a local newspaper as a hobby and as a way to earn a little extra money. These light and uplifting columns usually focused on farming and rural life.

When Wilder finally sat down to write the story of her childhood, she was more than 60 years old. Before she wrote her first book, she had only written newspaper columns. She had never thought of writing a children's book. Wilder did not go to school to learn how to write, nor did she take any creative writing classes. Nevertheless, she wanted to record the memories of her childhood and to portray a part of American life that was quickly disappearing. Would anyone want to read about her life? She soon found out the answer: a resounding yes. After the publication of her first book, *Little House in the Big Woods*, readers responded positively. They wrote letters to Wilder, asking to read more. Over the next 11 years,

Above is an 1867 illustration of a pioneer's home. Laura Ingalls and her family may have lived in a cabin quite like this.

Wilder wrote the nine books that make up the Little House series, five of which received the distinguished Newbery Honor award. She was 65 years old when her first book was published.

The success of her books surprised Wilder, and she remained grateful to her many fans. Although she became a famous author, she continued to live a quiet country life, and remained on the farm where she and her husband had lived for so many years. She still followed the philosophies by which she had lived her entire life. In 1947, in a letter addressed to the "children," written in response to her fans, Wilder wrote:

The "Little House" books are stories of long ago. The way we live and your schools are much different now, so many changes have made living and learning easier. But the real things haven't changed. It is still best to be honest and truthful; to make the most of what we have; to be happy with simple pleasures and to be cheerful and have courage when things go wrong.[1]

The Little House books are a source both of history and entertainment for children today. Written in the third person point of view, they are semi-autobiographical: Laura Ingalls is the star of the books. Readers follow her journey from a spunky five-year-old to an independent, strong-willed young woman.

Since the Little House books were first published, they have never gone out of print, and they continue to have strong sales. Translated into more than 40 languages, they are popular around the world. There is also a growing, multimillion-dollar franchise of Laura Ingalls Wilder merchandise, which includes cookbooks, trivia books, calendars, craft books, dishes, and diaries. There are several additional spin-off book series, and the successful long-running television show, *Little House on the Prairie,* continues to air in reruns.

The Little House books are considered classics of American children's literature. They remain widely read, primarily by girls ages 8–12, but they also delight many boys and adults, as well. Millions of readers around the world cherish the Little House books for their charming portrayal of Laura Ingalls and her endearing family. Although the books are considered historical fiction, they are based on the real-life adventures of the Ingalls family. The experiences of Wilder's childhood, the setting of the

American West, and the hardships and triumphs of her family helped shape Wilder as a writer and provided material for her books.

In the late nineteenth century, when Laura Ingalls Wilder was growing up, much of America was covered by wilderness. When she was a child, the Ingalls family lived in the woods, with the nearest town seven miles away. This painting shows settlers traveling by covered wagon in the far west.

2

Westward Bound

IN THE LATE nineteenth century, America was a much different place from what it is now. In many areas, wilderness stretched for miles, with trees so thick and numerous they sometimes blocked out the sky. In the western part of Wisconsin, where Wilder was born, miles of thick forest often separated one town from the next. Elm, oak, ash, maple, and basswood trees towered toward the sky, and panthers, bear, wolves, and deer roamed the woods.

Laura and her family referred to the place where they lived as the Big Woods, although technically, the Big Woods are in Minnesota, running from St. Cloud in the north to Mankato in the south. The Ingalls family lived near the border of Wisconsin and Minnesota. The nearest town was Pepin, 7 miles (more than 11 kilometers) away, where Laura's father sometimes went to trade furs or stock up on supplies, such as sugar or coffee. For the first year of her life, Laura lived in a small log cabin with her parents, Charles and Caroline Ingalls, and her sister, Mary.

Laura's parents were both Wisconsin pioneers. Their families had moved from the East, where much of the land was already settled, to the West, where they hoped to find large spreads of land to farm and claim as their own. Laura's father, Charles Ingalls, was born in Cuba, New York, in a rural area in the southwestern part of the state. A bright, blue-eyed boy, Charles was high spirited and curious; he always liked to learn new things. He grew up with eight brothers and sisters, and when he was nine years old, his family moved to Illinois, then north to Wisconsin. From the time he was young, Charles worked alongside his family on the farm. He learned to be a skilled carpenter, trapper, hunter, and farmer. Although he worked hard, Charles also enjoyed social gatherings, and he often played the fiddle for his family and friends at dances, weddings, and other events.

Laura's mother, Caroline Lake Quiner, was born on the Wisconsin frontier, but her parents were originally from Connecticut. When Caroline was five years old, her father drowned in a shipwreck on Lake Michigan. Caroline's mother tried to raise her family alone, but they soon ran out of food and fuel, and they had to rely on the help of neighbors to get them through the harsh winters. Three years after her father's death, Caroline's mother moved the family to a farm along the Oconomowoc River, where they raised bees for honey and farmed chickens and cows. She married a farmer one year later. Caroline's mother had been a teacher before she was married, and Caroline herself became a teacher when she was 16 years old. Many years later, Laura followed in the footsteps of her mother and grandmother.

Charles and Caroline lived on opposite sides of the Oconomowoc River, but they knew each other from church, parties, and dances. They often walked along the river together. On February 1, 1860, they were married. The Ingalls and Quiner families actually joined together three times. Caroline's brother Henry and Charles's sister Polly were married a year before Charles and Caroline. Then, a year after the wedding of Charles and Caroline, Uncle Peter, who was Charles's brother, married Aunt Eliza, who was Caroline's sister.

Caroline stopped teaching after she was married, because in those days only single women were allowed to teach. Caroline and Charles were a good match and well suited to the pioneer life. They were independent and resilient, and they passed those characteristics on to Laura. Charles's restlessness would eventually lead them west, and Caroline's level-headed nature would help them to create a warm, stable home no matter where they chose to live. Charles was jovial, outgoing, and adventurous, and Caroline was quiet and gentle.

Charles and Caroline bought an 80-acre plot in the Big Woods, not far from where Charles's parents had recently moved. They shared the land with friends named Henry and Polly Quiner. Life in the Big Woods could get lonely, and neighbors were scarce, so it was nice to have family nearby. Charles and Henry built two log cabins, one for each family, and they began clearing the land for crops. This was a difficult job because there were many trees and much vegetation.

During the time that Charles and Caroline were building a home and getting ready to start a family, the United States was divided in war. The Civil War had started in 1861, when 11 southern slave states declared their secession (their official withdrawal from the United States) and formed the Confederate States of America. The federal government, which was called the Union, opposed slavery and rejected the South's secession. The war tore the nation apart. By the time it ended, in 1865, more than 620,000 soldiers had been killed. Two of Charles's brothers fought for the Union, and one of Caroline's brothers was killed in the Battle of Shiloh in 1862.

For the most part, the war was far away from the rural setting of the Big Woods. Like many pioneers, Charles and Caroline were concerned about caring for farm animals, clearing land, hunting, tending crops, and storing food. They also had to think about taking care of their new family. Charles and Caroline had their first child, Mary Amelia, in 1865, toward the end of the Civil War. Two years later, Laura Elizabeth was born. Named after Charles's mother, Laura had brown hair and blue eyes like her father.

Most people in America at this time lived under depressed economic conditions. Jobs were scarce in the cities, and the farmers were not paid very much for their crops. Discouraged by the prospect of farming in Wisconsin, Charles believed that the family would be better off in the West. As more people settled near the Big Woods, Charles began to feel crowded in: "Wild animals would not stay in a county where there were so many people. Pa did not like to stay either." (*Little House in the Big Woods*, p. 2) Caroline was skeptical about leaving, but Charles convinced her that this was a good plan. He wanted to go to Kansas, where he had heard that the land was open and good for farming. In 1868,

Charles sold the farm to a Swedish settler named Gustaf Gustafson, and he and Caroline began to prepare for the big move west.

For many years, Americans were slow to settle the land west of the Mississippi River. The Louisiana Purchase and other land acquisitions had enlarged U.S territory, but much of the vast land in the West was still unsettled. When the Civil War ended in 1865, thousands of soldiers and civilians decided to see what lay beyond the great Mississippi River, which divided the East from the West.

The federal government's creation of the Homestead Act of 1862 was the biggest draw to the West. It basically said that any citizen could claim 160 acres of land for free, as long as certain conditions were met. For instance, the homesteader had to register his claim officially at a land office, a house had to be built on the claim, and the land needed to be plowed and farmed. If the government requirements were met after five years, then the land would become the homesteader's property. More than 270 million acres in America were opened up to citizens.

Thousands of settlers, including bachelors, families, freed slaves, single women, and newly arrived immigrants, migrated to the West.[2] Charles Ingalls also wanted the opportunity to become a homesteader, and he often sang one of the more popular songs of the time, "For Uncle Sam Is Rich Enough to Give Us All a Farm!"

On a cold winter day in 1869, when Lake Pepin was frozen solid, Charles, Caroline, Mary, and Laura left the Big Woods. Family and friends came to say good-bye. The Ingalls family set out in a covered wagon pulled by a team of oxen; the wagon's white canvas top protected their belongings. They packed books, clothes, dishes, bedding, and Charles's fiddle. The wagon, which was about 4 feet wide and from 10 to 12 feet in length, served as their moving home. It was called a prairie schooner, because the white canvas looked like the sails of a schooner ship. Jack, the Ingalls family's bulldog, trotted along under the wagon and helped protect them from wolves and horse thieves.

On the long and dangerous journey west, the Ingalls family crossed Minnesota, went south through Iowa and Missouri, and then west into Kansas. Years later, Wilder recorded the trip in her third book, *Little House on the Prairie*. Although she was too young to remember most of the journey, she heard the stories from her parents and sister many times, and these stories left a lasting impression. When Wilder wrote the Little House series, she and her family became the characters in the book. All of Wilder's work was semiautobiographical; she always wrote from her own and her families' experiences in the West.

The Ingalls family drove for miles without seeing another person, and it was difficult to cross over flooded creeks and rivers in the wagon. There were other dangers, too: wolves roamed the prairies. In the evenings, however, when the family gathered around the campfire and Charles played his fiddle, Laura and Mary felt safe. Wilder described how different the prairie was from the wooded setting they were used to: "There was only the enormous, empty prairie, with grasses blowing in waves of light and shadow across it, and the great blue sky above it, and birds flying up from it and singing with joy because the sun was rising. And on the whole enormous prairie there was no sign that any other human being had ever been there." (*Little House on the Prairie*, p. 38) Gophers, meadowlarks, and rabbits dotted the landscape and entertained the girls.

Eventually, the Ingalls family reached Kansas. Once they crossed the Verdigris River, they came to the small town of

Independence. After they continued for about 13 miles, they stopped on open prairie land that looked good for farming. Walnut Creek ran through the land, breaking up the flat stretch. The Ingalls family was in Rutland Township, in Montgomery County, Kansas. It seemed as if no one was around for miles; however, the family soon realized that the land was part of the Osage Diminished Reserve, home to the Osage Indians.

Settlers were rapidly displacing the Osage Indians, along with other Native American tribes. In the nineteenth century, many white Americans believed in the concepts of westward expansion and manifest destiny. Manifest destiny was the idea that Americans had a right and a mission to expand their civilization, culture, and institutions across the continent. It was this belief that caused many settlers to battle Native Americans and remove them from their land.

In 1830, the Congress of the United States passed the Indian Removal Act; but many Americans were against it, among them Tennessee congressman and folk hero Davy Crockett. The Act gave the government the right to remove Native Americans from their homes and relocate them to land that was further west. One of the most devastating and well-known examples of this was the Trail of Tears in 1836. Thousands of Cherokee, including women, children, and the elderly, were held in camps and then sent on a forced march from Georgia to Oklahoma; it is estimated that some 4,000 people died as a result.

As more settlers moved in, the Native Americans were pushed farther and farther west, and their land was greatly diminished. The federal government relocated Native Americans to Indian reservations, parcels of land set aside for specific tribes. The Osage Indians had originally lived along the Osage River in Missouri during the early 1800s,

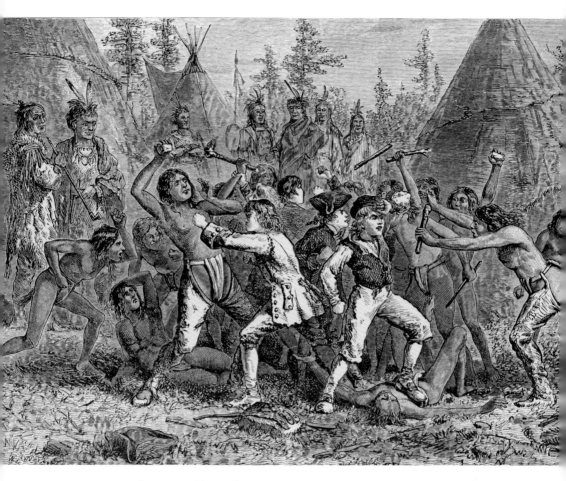

As more settlers moved into the West, Native Americans were often pushed out of the homes. One way the settlers justified this was by say-ing that the Native Americans were savages, as demonstrated by their depiction in the 1883 illustration above.

but with the arrival of settlers, they gave up their land and moved west. Now Montgomery County was a part of their reservation. Close to 9 million acres in size, it was the last major Indian reservation in the state.

The Ingalls family settled on the land illegally, because Charles had not filed a claim at the land office. At first, it seemed as if there was so much available land that no one would even notice them. Charles began to build a house. He cut trees for logs, dragged them to the house site, and raised the walls. He used a horse-drawn plow to break up the grassy prairie into fields, and Caroline turned the log house into a cozy home. The family lived in a one-room cabin. Laura and Mary slept in one bed, and Charles and Caroline slept in the other bed. There were many scary nights for Laura, such as the time a pack of wolves surrounded the cabin, or when harsh winds wailed against the walls. Mostly, however, she felt safe with her family.

In 1870, Caroline gave birth to another girl. The baby was named after her mother, and they all called her Carrie. In telling her family's story, Wilder included Carrie for the first time as a character in *Little House in the Big Woods*. Carrie did not appear in *Little House on the Prairie*, even though she was born during the events of this book. Wilder had not known at the time that she would write an entire series.

Although the prairie seemed vast and empty, the Ingalls family soon came into contact with other white settlers on the reservation. Their closest pioneer neighbors lived a few miles away. They included the Scotts, a couple with no children, and Mr. Edwards, a bachelor.

The Native Americans usually camped by the river. Sometimes they walked along the trail that ran past the Ingalls family's cabin, and occasionally, they visited the house, wanting food or tobacco. As more settlers pushed onto the land, the Native American tribes lost their hunting grounds, and many were hungry. Wilder recalled that her mother was frightened and uneasy in the presence of the Osage, but her father seemed more hopeful that the settlers and Indian tribes could live peacefully alongside each other. After they encountered the Native Americans, many settlers realized that they were not the "savages" they had thought them to be. Unfortunately, throughout the nineteenth century, the ideas that the indigenous people were bloodthirsty, backward savages dominated popular belief. These ideas were heightened by sensational frontier stories.

As more and more settlers began to arrive and set up homes on the Osage Indian Reservation, tensions rose. The settlers were crowding the Osage's hunting land, destroying trails, and driving away the wildlife. There were no actual battles, but Wilder, who was three at the time, recalled in *Little House on the Prairie* the nights when the Osage held powwows (ceremonies) down in the valley. The noise of drumming and their terrifying war cries filled the tiny cabin. The Osage were trying to decide whether they should leave or declare war on the settlers.

Wilder wrote about the family's encounters with the Native Americans in *Little House in the Prairie* and in *Little House in the Big Woods*. Both books have been challenged

Did you know...

The dramatic television series *Little House on the Prairie* aired from 1974 to 1983. Set in Walnut Grove, Minnesota, this popular show was a loose adaptation of Wilder's books. Several fictional characters in the television series, such as Albert, the adopted son, were not in Wilder's books. Featuring Michael Landon as Charles Ingalls and Melissa Gilbert as Laura Ingalls, *Little House on the Prairie* became one of the most successful hour-long series in network history, running eight seasons. It currently airs as reruns.

The stories of Wilder's life were the inspiration for the popular television series Little House on the Prairie. *Above, the cast of the show poses together.*

in schools as racially offensive, and people have accused Wilder of using stereotypes to describe the Native Americans. Others, in defense of the books, argue that Wilder was writing during a particular time when this prejudiced view was the common perception. They also point out that she was trying to show everything through the eyes of a child.

We cannot be sure exactly how Charles and Caroline viewed the Osage. Although Charles defended the Native Americans in conversations with the other settlers and believed they were peaceable, he was also waiting for the day when the Osage would give up the land. A railroad company wanted to buy up the Osage Indian Reservation, and at first offered the tribes an insulting price of 18 cents an acre. This treaty was blocked in the U.S. Senate. Eventually, the U.S. government paid the Osage $1.25 per acre for their Kansas land, and they relocated to a new reservation in Oklahoma. They rode away on their horses and ponies one day, never to see their land again.

Charles and Caroline were also expressing doubts at this stage about staying in Kansas. When settlers arrived from the East, they were excited to claim their "free" homestead land, but they quickly realized how difficult life was on the prairie. In addition to the hard work, isolation, and growing tension with the Native Americans, there were also illnesses and harsh weather conditions. Wilder wrote about a time when the entire Ingalls family fell sick with malaria—which they probably caught from the thick swarms of mosquitoes prevalent on the prairie—and Dr. Tann, a black doctor to the Native Americans, who gave them medicine and took care of them.

One day, the family received a letter from Wisconsin from Gustaf Gustafson, who said he could not finish paying for the land in Wisconsin and wanted Charles to take it back. This gave them another reason to leave Kansas. Although Caroline was sorry to leave behind all that they had worked for, it seemed like the right thing to do. They loaded up the wagon once again, and this time they headed east. When they returned to their cabin in the Big Woods in the spring of 1871, Wilder was four years old. Her memories of the Big Woods were rich and deep, and she would one day write about them in her first published book, *Little House in the Big Woods*.

The illustration above, created in 1869, is titled "Emigrants crossing the plains." Like the Ingalls family, many Americans moved around the country throughout the nineteenth century, trying to find good land where they could farm and build new lives.

3

Seeing the
World Twice

WILDER'S MEMORIES OF the Big Woods were warm and pleasant. Her parents gave her and her sisters much attention and provided them with a stable, loving home. Although the winters in Wisconsin were severe and the work seemed endless, inside the little log cabin, Laura felt protected and loved: "All alone in the wild 'Big Woods,' and the snow, and the cold, the little log house was warm and snug and cozy. Charles and Caroline and Mary and Laura and Baby Carrie were comfortable and happy there, especially at night." (*Little House in the Big Woods*, p. 38)

Laura felt very close to her father, who called her his "little half-pint of sweet cider half drunk up." (*Little House in the Big Woods*, p. 33) Charles passed on to Laura his sense of adventure, as well as his love of nature and the outdoors. In her books, Wilder depicted her father as fearless and strong. She also portrayed him as a gentle, reasonable man. In one scene in *Little House in the Big Woods*, he does not shoot a deer because of its beauty: "It was a perfect shot. But he was so beautiful, he looked so strong and free and wild, that I couldn't kill him. I sat there and looked at him, until he bounded away into the dark woods." (*Little House in the Big Woods*, p. 233)

Wilder described herself as more like her father than her mother, whereas Mary was more like Caroline. Blond and blue-eyed, Mary was obedient and reserved, but Laura was a tomboy. She liked to play outside and was sometimes scolded for not being ladylike. In *Little House in the Big Woods*, Wilder wrote about feeling jealous of Mary: "Mary was a good little girl who always kept her dress clean and neat and minded her manners. Mary had lovely golden curls. . . . Mary looked very good and sweet, unrumpled and clean, sitting on the board beside Laura. Laura did not think it was fair." (*Little House in the Big Woods*, p. 175) Like most siblings, the sisters sometimes squabbled, but most of the time they got along. They played together with rag dolls and watched over their baby sister, Carrie. Sometimes, their mother cut out paper dolls for them. Their father even built them playhouses.

Try to imagine a time before fast food, computers, stereos, shopping malls, or telephones. The Ingalls family, like all pioneer families, did everything for themselves: They grew their own food, sewed their own clothes, and built their own furniture. Trips to town were rare; to survive in the pioneer days, people had to be self-sufficient. Charles cut wood for fuel and cleared away the trees to plant crops and gardens. He hunted deer and bear, and then he smoked and salted the meat so the family could save it for the long, hard winters. Charles also trapped minks, foxes, and wolves, and he often traded the furs for fabric and staples in town. He also butchered a hog every year, which was an all-day event that Wilder described in *Little House on the Prairie.* Nothing was easy; Charles even made his own bullets for his gun.

Caroline worked as hard as her husband. During this time, women had very few choices. Although there were a handful of adventurous, independent women who went west to claim their own homesteads, most women married and raised a family. In addition to the cooking and many chores in the house, Caroline also helped Charles with the outdoor work. She worked in the garden and helped butcher meat and cure it for the winter. Caroline also made sure that she taught her daughters the skills that women were expected to have at that time: cleaning the house, washing laundry, ironing, mending and sewing, baking and cooking, and churning butter, a chore that Laura liked.

Charles was usually away working in the fields or hunting during the mornings and afternoons, and Laura looked forward to his return at the end of the day. In the evenings, the family gathered around the fire and listened to Charles as he told stories and played the fiddle. The settlers did not have CDs, records, or stereo systems, so people created their own music. They played the fiddle, harmonica, guitar, banjo, or makeshift instruments, such as a washboard. Charles played songs like "Yankee Doodle," "Marching Through Georgia," "Irish Washerwoman," "Devil's Hornpipe," and "Arkansas Traveler." To Laura's delight, he got down on his hands and knees to play the role of "Mad Dog" and chase her. Her mother usually sat in the rocking chair and sewed, and sometimes she read Bible stories to the girls. Caroline also read aloud from popular novels such as *Millbank* or *Norwood*, and from newspapers and church papers. One of the girls' favorite books belonged to their father: *A Description of Man and Nature in the Polar and Equatorial Regions of the Globe.*

Wilder's parents placed a strong emphasis on education and reading. Between her father's love of storytelling and her mother's love of books, Wilder learned the power of the story. In the *Little House* series, she retold many of her father's stories, which were always entertaining and often contained some kind of message or lesson. Charles and Caroline enrolled the girls in school whenever they could. The Barry Corner School was one-half mile down the road from their home in the Big Woods. Mary, who was six, was old enough to attend. When Mary came home at the end of the day, she showed Laura the words she had learned, and soon Laura could read, too.

The winters in the Big Woods were the most difficult times, with the wind howling against the cabin walls: "Laura listened to the wind in the 'Big Woods.' All around the house the wind went crying as though it were lost in the dark and the cold. The wind sounded frightened." (*Little House in the Big Woods*, p. 107) Charles and Caroline worked hard to make sure they prepared for the cold winters, but the season was also filled with festivity. Christmas was a joyous time in their home, as Wilder described in *Little House in the Big Woods*. In one of the more memorable passages, she explained how her mother boiled a pot of molasses and sugar and then showed the girls how to pour the syrup over a pan of fresh snow. They made designs with the hot syrup, and later the syrup hardened into sweet candy.

As more people moved in, the isolated woods was transformed. Charles began to feel restless and closed in again, and he talked to Caroline about selling their land and heading west for a second time. Caroline liked living near people and felt reluctant to leave, but Charles insisted that the West promised good land deals and economic opportunities.

For a second time, Charles sold his farm in the Big Woods. When the Ingalls family headed west this time, Uncle Peter and Aunt Eliza came too. It was bitter cold when the two families left on February 7, 1874, Laura's seventh birthday. They had waited until the ice was thick enough to cross the Mississippi River.

Peter and Eliza stopped to settle in eastern Minnesota, but Charles, Caroline, Mary, Laura, and Carrie continued to travel west. On the way, Laura saw her first train speed across the plains. The prairie was green, with bright wildflowers. At night, they camped along creeks and sat around a fire. Caroline prepared meals, and Charles played his fiddle, happy to be on the move again.

The Ingalls family finally stopped in Walnut Grove, Minnesota, part of Redwood County. Although the town had only a few buildings and houses, there were railroad tracks that had been laid the year before, which was a good sign that the town would grow. Charles learned about a 172-acre plot that was for sale about a mile north of town. The land looked promising. It was a vast prairie, with a stream called Plum Creek and a little sod house. The house, which was also called a dugout because it was dug into the ground, had only one room that was about the size of a wagon. The thick walls were made of earth, and the roof was made of willow boughs with sod laid over them. Since grass grew on the roof, the house blended in with the prairie ground, except for the stovepipe sticking up above ground.

The Ingalls family settled into their new home. In the spring, Charles plowed the fields for wheat, and Laura and Mary helped their mother turn the dugout into a nice house. When they were not doing chores, Laura and Mary played along Plum Creek. They fished and waded in the water. Willow trees shaded the cool, clean creek, and wild plums grew all around it.

The house was close to town, which Caroline liked. There were enough residents in Walnut Grove to have a church and a school. Caroline and Charles helped to organize the Union Congregational Church with the help of a missionary minister, Reverend Edward Alden. Both Charles and Caroline had grown up in religious households, where prayer and reading the Bible were regular activities in the home.

Walnut Grove, Minnesota, may be the most recognized name of all the towns Wilder wrote about in her books. It is the setting of the television series *Little House on the Prairie*. Although the show suggests that the family lived there until Laura was an adult, in reality, they lived there only a few years.

Laura and her sisters attended school in Walnut Grove. Schooling for the girls was somewhat sporadic, depending on where they were living and if there was a school nearby. A bright student, Laura loved to read and to learn as much as she loved to climb trees, ride ponies, and wade in creeks. She was a quick learner and curious to know more; she also enjoyed playtime. Unlike Mary, who was quiet and reserved, Laura did not worry about looking ladylike. Spunky, active, and competitive, Laura liked to run and

Above is a family sitting outside their dugout house in Oklahoma. The sod house that the Ingalls family had in Walnut Grove might have looked very much like this one.

play, and she was never too timid to join in the boys' games, like "Ante-I-Over" and "Pullaway."

The school was small, and the children wrote on their own pieces of slate. Most of the other students were the children of homesteaders. Like Laura and Mary, they came from poor families. There were a few town children who wore nicer clothes, like Nellie and Willie Owens, whose parents owned a store. Laura thought that Nellie and Willie were spoiled and mean. Later, when Wilder wrote about them in *On the Banks of Plum Creek*, she changed their last name to Oleson.

Summer and fall were pleasant on the prairie, but the winter brought snow, sleet, and furious wind. Blizzards were common. Stories circulated about people who got lost and froze to death just a few steps from their doors. Laura and Mary could not go to school in weather like this, so their mother taught them their lessons at home.

When winter finally ended, Charles began to build his family a real house. Buying everything on credit, he went into town to find yellow pine lumber and glass for the windows. Charles was counting on a large profit, since

Did you know...

The character of Nellie Oleson was based on three different girls from Laura's life. Nellie was actually a combination of Nellie Owens, Genevieve Masters, and Stella Gilbert. Nellie Owens, who had a young brother named Willie and whose parents ran a local general store in Walnut Grove, was the main basis for Nellie in *On the Banks of Plum Creek*. The Nellie who appears in *Little Town on the Prairie* is based on Genevieve Masters, who wore pretty clothes and had beautiful golden ringlets, just as Nellie Oleson did. The Nellie in *These Happy Golden Years* is based on Stella Gilbert, a poor girl who lived on a claim near De Smet. Although she was poor, she was beautiful, and she had her eye on Almanzo.

the wheat fields were already green and beautiful, and he planned to pay the storeowners back once he could harvest the wheat. He surprised Caroline with a black iron cookstove so she would not have to cook in the fireplace.

Everything seemed to be going well, but then disaster struck. One day, glittery, immense clouds whirled in the sky and descended upon the fields. These were not just clouds. They were grasshoppers: swarms of millions and millions of grasshoppers. The grasshoppers devoured everything in sight, including the wheat crop, the plum thicket, and the garden. They ate whatever they could, even clothing and the paint on buildings. Grasshopper "lakes" were reported around the area, which were filled three inches deep with grasshoppers. Farms all around Minnesota were destroyed, and many disgusted farmers left their land and moved away.

Later, Wilder wrote about the devastating experience in *On the Banks of Plum Creek*: "The cloud was hailing grasshoppers. The cloud *was* grasshoppers. Their bodies hid the sun and made darkness. Their thin, large wings gleamed and glittered. The rasping whirring of their wings filled the air and they hit the ground and the house with the noise of a hailstorm." (*On the Banks of Plum Creek*, p. 195)

Although many farmers left the area, the Ingalls family decided to try farming again the next season. Instead of struggling through another cold winter on the prairie, the family moved to town for the season. They found a little house for rent behind the church. Mary and Laura could easily walk to school. On November 1, 1875, Caroline gave birth to a baby boy. They named him Charles Frederic Ingalls after his father, and they called him Freddy.

When the snow melted, the family returned to its home on Plum Creek. Once again, Charles sowed another wheat crop, hoping for the best. Unfortunately, the grasshoppers had laid eggs in the ground, and when they hatched, they destroyed everything. They ate crops, grass, and leaves on trees. Everything the Ingalls family had worked for was ruined. The only choice now was to leave the farm and head east. Laura saw that her father was deeply disappointed to be leaving their home, and she felt the same way.

The Ingalls family moved to South Troy, Minnesota, to live with Uncle Peter and Aunt Eliza for the summer. The trip was long, and baby Freddy was often sick, but once they arrived, Laura was happy to see her cousins. Peter and Eliza had five children, and the house was crowded with the two families. The children helped with the many chores. One of Laura's favorite jobs was to watch over the cows. During the day, she and her cousins made sure that the cows did not wander too far away or eat the hay that was saved for winter. At sunset, they led the cows back to the stable.

At the end of the summer, in 1876, the family faced another tragedy when baby Freddy died at the age of nine months. He had always been sickly. In those days, it was difficult to get medicine, and many cures had not yet been discovered. Death was a part of pioneer life; no one was sheltered from it, but everyone in the family was deeply saddened by Freddy's death.

The Ingalls family was on the move. Next, they went to Burr Oak, Iowa, to live with the Steadmans, whom they knew from church in Walnut Grove. The Steadmans managed a hotel, and they offered the Ingalls family living space and a part of the profits in exchange for work. Caroline and Charles were not happy about the saloon next door to the hotel. They did not think it was a good place for three girls to grow up. The grasshopper invasion had put them in a difficult financial situation, however, and they needed to take whatever work they could get.

Burr Oak was a much older town than Walnut Grove. It was a major stop on the westward journey, and it had once been a very busy and exciting place. By the time the Ingalls family arrived, the town had quieted down, but it still attracted many visitors. Guests constantly came and went. A night's lodging cost 25 cents, and a meal cost the same.

Laura was nine years old when the family lived in Burr Oak. In her eyes, the hotel, which was three stories high and had 11 rooms, was a grand and exciting place. She helped with chores around the hotel, like cleaning and washing dishes. The two families shared a space downstairs, and when the hotel became too crowded, Laura's parents found a rental house on the edge of town, next to woods filled with oak trees. Laura enjoyed living there. Once again, they had a cow, and she was responsible for taking it out to pasture every morning and bringing it back at night.

Caroline gave birth to Grace Pearl on May 23, 1877. Now there were four girls in the Ingalls family. To one of the town's residents, Mrs. Starr, this seemed like more than enough daughters. Laura once overheard Mrs. Starr explaining to Caroline that since her own daughters were grown and lived far away, she was very lonely. She wanted Laura to live with her and to be her daughter. It must have scared Laura to hear this, and to think that she could be sent away from her beloved parents and sisters. Of course, Caroline would never consider such an absurd offer. She just listened politely, and then told Mrs. Starr that she and Charles could not give up Laura.

When the Ingalls family decided it was time to return to Walnut Grove the next year, they were surprised to see how much the town had grown. Charles found a job in a general store, and he did carpentry work around town. To bring in extra money, he also opened a butcher shop. In the spring,

Charles bought a lot behind a hotel owned by the Masters family and built a small house. It felt good for the family to be together in their own home, without having to share the space with others.

The girls attended school again, and many of the same students were there, including Nellie Owens and Genevieve Masters, who came from New York. Like Nellie, Genevieve Masters was also spoiled and snooty. She later became part of the inspiration for the Nellie Oleson character in Wilder's novels. Nellie and Genevieve did not like each other, and they fought over which one was the most popular. Laura did not get along with either girl, but she had other friends. She enjoyed school and was one of the best spellers in the class. At recess, she was a natural leader, but she played easily with the other children. Mary thought Laura was too wild, but the boys saw how athletic and quick Laura was, and they wanted her to play in their baseball games for the season.

On Sundays, like most pioneer families, the Ingalls family attended church. They belonged to the Congregational church, where they went in the mornings. In the afternoons, the girls also went to the Methodist church services. One Sunday, the Methodists announced a contest, offering a prize to the child who could recite from memory the golden texts and central truths from the Bible, which equaled 104 biblical verses. Laura and another student, Howard Ensign, recited all of the verses without any mistakes. The prize was a Bible, but there was only one. The minister's wife told Laura that they would order a new one, a fancier edition, if she could wait a while, and Laura was happy to wait for it.

When school ended for the summer, Laura worked for Mrs. Masters at the hotel. She washed dishes, cleaned the hotel, and babysat, earning 50 cents a week. The Ingalls family was still struggling, and every little bit helped. Charles did not earn much at his various jobs, and the family had very little money. Laura felt that she could not refuse when Mrs. Masters offered her a job to help a sick relative who lived two miles away in the country. She went to stay with Sadie Hurley, the woman who was ill, and although Hurley was kind, Laura missed her family and was thankful when she could return home again.

Tragedy struck the Ingalls family once again, in 1879. Mary suddenly grew ill; she felt a fierce pain in her head and ran a high fever. The doctors called her illness "brain fever," which could have meant many kinds of sicknesses at that time, but it was probably scarlet fever. As Mary recovered, her eyesight began to grow dimmer and dimmer. The doctors said that the nerves in Mary's eyes were dying. Then, the terrible day arrived when Mary could not see at all. She would be blind for the rest of her life.

Laura watched Mary patiently accept her fate. The family showed her support and love, and Mary's own quiet strength also pulled her through. Charles told Laura that now she must help Mary, that she must be "her sister's eyes," and Laura took this duty very seriously. Laura described as much as she could to Mary: the landscape, people, color, and light. She told her stories and found the right words to capture the way things looked. As Laura acted as her sister's guide, this may have helped to shape her as a writer. She became good at paying attention to the world around her, as well as describing what she saw. Perhaps this was the start of a lifelong habit of looking closely and seeing everything twice: once for herself and once for her sister. Years later, in her books, Wilder brought the Big Woods and the prairie to life through her vivid descriptions and details.

In the American West in the nineteenth century, railroads were big business. They were the best way to travel across the large, relatively unpopulated country, and the fastest way to ship goods from farmer to market. In the late 1870s, Charles Ingalls took a job with a railroad company store in order to support his family.

4

The Railroad Boom

THE INGALLS FAMILY continued to have money trouble. Charles and Caroline were in debt, with no savings to buy land. One day, Charles's sister Docia visited from Wisconsin, passing through Walnut Grove on her way west to meet her husband, Hiram Forbes, who was a contractor working for the railroad. Docia offered Charles a job, and he happily accepted. He would be a bookkeeper and manage the company store. Laura recalled that her mother was sad to leave Walnut Grove. She finally agreed, but only on the condition that Charles promised that they would not move again.

Although moving to the West was filled with tribulations, Charles still felt hopeful about finding a spread of farmland to homestead. The Dakota Territory seemed like a promising place to go. As the northernmost part of the Louisiana Purchase, it had become an organized territory in 1861 and included most of Wyoming and Montana, as well as what would become the two Dakotas. The Dakota Territory was much less settled than Minnesota, with plenty of government homesteads still available. In 1879, the Ingalls family settled into what is now South Dakota, which did not become a state until 1889.

The Dakota Territory was one of the last portions of the frontier, but even this area was quickly being settled. During the Great Dakota boom of the late 1870s, a wave of migration swept into the Dakota Territory. Thousands of pioneers came, setting up homes and farms, as well as stores, grain elevators, lumberyards, and other businesses.

The railroads were the major draw, and they meant more work and more people. Created in the early nineteenth century, railroads brought one of the most dramatic changes to America. Through them the West was linked to the East. Goods and mail could be delivered and shipped, and people could travel more easily, so towns sprang up along the railroad lines. Freight trains brought in goods from the East, and the farmers could rely on the trains to ship their crops back to the eastern markets. Railroads symbolized economic security and progress.

For the Native Americans, however, the railroads brought disaster. As more settlers arrived, the Native Americans were drastically displaced. They lost their land and hunting grounds to the settlers. On their travels to the Dakota Territory, the Ingalls family passed by old Indian trails and buffalo paths, but the huge herds of buffalo were already long gone. It was a sad image that stayed with Wilder for many years. Her father told her that the buffalo had once covered the land but was now almost extinct. In fact, in 1789, 60 million bison had roamed the plains. There were immense herds of tens of thousands of buffalo as far as the eye could see.

By the time the Ingalls family moved to the Dakota Territory in 1879, the total number of buffalo in the United States was less than a few hundred, and by 1894, the number was down to about 25. Millions and millions of buffalo were destroyed from 1830 to the 1870s.[3] Professional hunters killed tens of thousands for robes, which were sold in eastern markets. A great number died because they lost their habitat: Settlers chopped down the trees that had been the bison's winter habitat, and then they built towns and railroads over the land. The settlers' horses and cattle also devoured the grazing lands and brought new diseases. The buffalo had been a great source of food, clothing, and spiritual power for the Native Americans.

Although the frontier was disappearing far more quickly than anyone had ever expected, these new towns were still very isolated. At the Silver Lake railroad camp, along the Big Sioux River, the Ingalls family lived in a small shanty apart from the bunkhouses where the railroad workers stayed. Charles worked as a bookkeeper and timekeeper for the Dakota Central crews. There were very few women in the camp, and Caroline made sure that the girls did not go near the bunkhouse. She did not approve of the fact that the men used rough language and drank. By the late fall, the construction work was finished, and the railroad men left Silver Lake. Charles thought his family would leave too, but the railroad surveyor offered him a job to stay in the camp over the winter and guard the supplies and equipment. Wilder wrote about these memories in her book, *By the Shores of Silver Lake.*

The Ingalls family moved into the surveyor's home, where they settled for the winter. At night, Charles played the fiddle and told stories, and the family read and played games such as checkers on a board that Charles had carved. Using the light of the kerosene lamp, they always read aloud so that Mary could hear the stories. Reading was a popular activity on the frontier; it was an escape from the hard workdays and one of the few sources of entertainment. People read whatever they could get their hands on: the Bible, classic literature, and month-old newspapers and magazines.

As winter turned to spring, more settlers arrived. Meanwhile, Charles searched for available land to homestead. One day, he came home and said that he had found the perfect place: 160 acres of homestead land that was just a mile from the town site of De Smet.

The Ingalls family was among the first settlers in De Smet and helped to build up the town. Charles built two store buildings, and at some point, he was also named Justice of the Peace. As the town grew, they built a general store, a hotel, a saloon, and they began a newspaper. When the last railroad track was laid, the trains started coming and leaving regularly, and more and more people came in from the East.

It was the end of the wide-open prairie; now things could never go back to the way they were. In 1806, President Thomas Jefferson had predicted that it would take a hundred generations to settle the land in the West, but by 1890, the frontier was already closed. Although Laura liked the new town of De Smet, she also felt sad about the changes. Her memories of settling in the West, as well as her love of the wilderness and untamed land, were a major part of her life. When she finally sat down to write many years later, it made sense that she turned to these memories.

The Ingalls family moved at first into a small shanty on the 160-acre homestead. There was a tremendous amount of work to be done. Charles dug a well, planted cotton-wood saplings, built a shelter for the horses and livestock, and broke ground with his plow for a garden. The family planted turnips, potatoes, beans, tomatoes, corn, and pumpkins, hoping to live off the land as much as they could. Laura helped her father on the farm, and she was not afraid of doing "men's work."

The Ingalls family attended the new Congregational Church, and Laura and Carrie went to school in De Smet. Laura made friends easily. She continued to play ball and throw snowballs with the boys, but she was now beginning to feel more pressure to behave "like a lady."

When the first winter came, no one in town was quite prepared. It began in mid-October with a fierce blizzard. Wilder later recalled a story about an old Sioux Indian who came into town to warn the settlers that a terrible winter was on its way. Charles moved the family into town to his store building, where they would be safer from the cold. For six months, a succession of blizzards swept over the town. Once, Laura and Carrie could hardly find their way home from school. Trains were delayed because the snow covered the tracks, and coal and food supplies grew low. The last sack of flour in town sold for $50, and the last sack of sugar sold for $1 a pound. School was closed, and the trains stopped.

This became known as the hard winter. There was no coal, so people began to burn lumber, but Charles did not want to do something so careless. Instead, Laura helped him twist hay into sticks, like a rope, and they burned this

*The Ingalls family were among the first settlers in the town of De Smet.
Prairie towns then were slapdash affairs, with the most important
buildings quickly built. Above is a photograph of the prairie town
of Garden City, Kansas, in 1885.*

in the stove. The temperature in their kitchen was barely
above freezing. Caroline was careful to conserve their
supplies, but they eventually ran out of everything: flour,
sugar, meat, and potatoes. During this time, George and
Maggie Masters and their new baby stayed with them.
Wilder later decided not to include the Masters family in
the book, *The Long Winter*, because she did not want to
take the focus away from her family.

Did you know...

There are many museums and historical sites dedicated to the memory of Laura Ingalls Wilder. Pepin, Wisconsin, celebrates Wilder's life every September with traditional music, craft demonstrations, a "Laura look-alike" contest, and a spelling bee. Kansas has designated Wilder's childhood home near Independence as a historic site, with a cabin modeled after the original Ingalls family home. In Walnut Grove, Minnesota, the Wilder Pageant is held each summer. This annual outdoor drama is based upon Wilder's life and is presented live on the banks of Plum Creek. In De Smet, South Dakota, several important buildings are open to visitors. These include the family homestead; a house in town built by Charles Ingalls; the Brewster School, where Wilder taught; and the surveyor's home in which the family lived between 1879 and 1880. De Smet is also home to the Laura Ingalls Wilder Memorial Society. In Mansfield, Missouri, where Wilder wrote the *Little House* books, the town holds an annual festival, turning back the clock to the late 1800s. In addition, the farmhouse that Laura and Almanzo built is open to visitors, and the Laura Ingalls Wilder–Rose Wilder Lane Museum, next door, contains many of Wilder's personal belongings, as well Charles's fiddle and Caroline's sewing machine. Other restored sites include the Masters Hotel at Burr Oak, Iowa, where the Ingalls family lived in 1876, and the Almanzo Wilder Home.

One day, Laura's classmate Cap Garland and a young homesteader, Almanzo Wilder, made a risky 12-mile journey to buy wheat for the starving townsfolk. After they brought the supply back, the storeowner in De Smet wanted to make a profit by selling the wheat for an inflated price. Charles and the other men pressured him to sell it for what he paid for it, and Cap and Almanzo were considered heroes.

In May, for the first time in four months, a train pulled in from the East. When the snow finally melted, the family returned to their homestead claim. Charles added two rooms to the house and plowed the fields. To earn money, he took construction jobs in town, and Laura also helped earn money by sewing at a dry goods store. She earned 25 cents an hour, which added up to $9 by the end of the summer.

Laura used her earnings to contribute to Mary's education. Like Laura, Mary had always loved school. Charles and Caroline wanted to give their daughter a chance to learn, so they took Mary by train to Vinton, Iowa, where she would attend the Iowa College for the Blind. Although Laura was sad to see her sister go, she also knew it was the best thing for her. At school, Mary studied history, chemistry, algebra, economy, and music. She played the piano and organ; she also mastered fancy work, which consisted of sewing, knitting, and weaving.

At Laura's school, the teacher was Miss Eliza Wilder, the sister of Almanzo, whom Laura would one day marry. Laura had a strong sense of justice and fairness, and she did not like her teacher because she thought Miss Wilder favored some students over others. Laura was also disappointed that Genevieve Masters had moved to De Smet and was in her class again; nevertheless, she continued to excel at school.

Laura liked history and writing the best. She had also started to write poetry during the hard winter, writing the poems in her neat handwriting and creating little homemade books. It still never crossed her mind to want to be a professional writer, which did not seem like a possibility for a pioneer, especially for a woman. She paid close attention to all that was around her, and one day these experiences would find their way into her books. Think about all of the changes she saw in America. The memories of her family's experiences in the West were deep and long lasting.

Above, a man and a boy sit in a two-horse buggy, in this photograph from 1865. When Laura Ingalls was a teacher, she lived about 12 miles away from her family. Her beau, Almanzo Wilder, picked her up in a buggy like this, in order to take her home for the weekends.

5

Teaching, Marriage, and Motherhood

LAURA CONTINUED TO be one of the top students at the De Smet School. Once, at a school event, she recited half of the story of American history. Her performance impressed many people, including Mr. Bouchie, who was the head of a small school about 12 miles south of De Smet. He offered Laura a teaching job for two months. In her book, *These Happy Golden Years*, Wilder wrote about this experience, but she called the character Mr. Brewster. It was a big change for Laura to go from being a student to being the teacher: "Only yesterday she was a schoolgirl; now she was a school teacher. This happened so suddenly." (*These Happy Golden Years*, p. 1) Laura was not yet

16 years old, which was the legal age for teaching, but Mr. Bouchie told her not to mention this to the superintendent.

Laura worked at the school during January and February for $20 a month; this was below the average rate, but the money would help her struggling family. She taught the five students in a small rural one-room schoolhouse, and she left her family to live with Mr. and Mrs. Bouchie closer to the school. This was not a pleasant experience, or an uncommon one. Mrs. Bouchie hated the frontier life, and she was depressed by the isolation: "At supper, no one said a word. The stillness was so sullen and hateful that Laura could not speak." (*These Happy Golden Years*, p. 21)

Frontier life was difficult, lonely, and often very boring. Imagine that your closest neighbors live several miles away, and that you have to drive a horse and buggy over barren, wild lands to visit them. Laura felt that Mrs. Bouchie was not very friendly, and she herself felt trapped at the Bouchie home and discouraged by her students. On the weekends, she was allowed to leave, but she did not expect her father to make the long journey to pick her up.

That first weekend, however, a buggy drove up. It was not her father, but the young homesteader Almanzo Wilder. Laura was surprised and happy to see him. Almanzo drove her back to her parents' home, which became the routine every week, although Laura was a little worried: "She hoped he did not think that she was expecting him to do it. Surely he was not thinking of . . . well, of maybe being her beau?" (*These Happy Golden Years*, p. 51) Laura was growing up, and young men were beginning to show an interest in her. She was attractive, intelligent, and independent.

Almanzo was the most persistent of all of her suitors, but he did not push her too hard. It was a quiet courtship. When he drove her home from the Bouchies' house, she thanked him, but she also told him that their rides would not continue after she was living back home again.

When the two months at Mr. Bouchie's school ended, Laura gave her earnings to her father and returned to school in De Smet. Her teacher, Professor Ven Owen, felt that Laura was his most promising student. She excelled at writing compositions and essays, but she also still liked to play with her friends. Laura went sledding, and once she and her friends skipped school so they could go to a new skating rink.

When Laura was back home with her parents, she still went riding with Almanzo, although she had told him that she would not. Almanzo owned a pair of Morgan horses and a driving buggy. Once, he brought a wild team, Skip and Barnum, and she had to run to jump into the buggy because the team could not be stopped. They rode all over, racing across the prairie. There was a time when Almanzo was also taking Stella Gilbert along with them on their rides, but Laura finally told him to make a choice. She wrote about the incident in *These Happy Golden Years*, but instead of Stella, Wilder used the character of Nellie Oleson.

One day, Laura and Almanzo talked about their names. Laura did not like the nicknames that Almanzo's family called him, like Manzo and Mannie. She decided to call him Manly instead. Almanzo had an older sister named Laura, and he admitted that he had never particularly liked the name. When she told him that her middle name was Elizabeth, he decided to call her Bessie.

While Laura was still finishing school, she took a job teaching at the Perry School, which was just a short walk from home. She had only three students. Laura also continued to take various sewing jobs to earn extra money, which she always gave to her family. With Laura and her father's combined earnings, they were able to buy a pump organ for

Mary. When Mary was home from the School for the Blind on summer vacations, she liked to play music.

Almanzo proposed, and Laura accepted the engagement ring, although in *The First Four Years*, she admitted that she was reluctant to marry a farmer. She knew it would be a hard life, with endless work and unstable finances. At the time of their engagement, Laura was 17 years old, and Almanzo was 27. It was acceptable then for a teenaged woman to get married, and it rarely happened on the prairie that a woman did not marry, although there were always exceptions. At this time in America, women could not yet vote, and there were few career choices for women other than teaching or raising a family.

Laura wanted to teach one more term of school before she married, and she agreed to teach at the Wilkens School, which meant that she would not be able to finish her own classes. Although Laura regretted that she did not complete high school, she knew that this was her last chance to teach. Once she was married, she would have to give up the position: only single women were allowed to be teachers at that time.

Laura and Almanzo were married on August 25, 1885. It was a quiet wedding: just the two of them at the Reverend Brown's house. The ceremony was short and quick, and they went back to her parents' house for dinner afterwards. During the ceremony, Laura had refused to say "obey" in her wedding vows, which was unusual for women in those days. Another way Wilder surprised people is when she used her maiden name of Ingalls, along with her husband's last name, when she wrote her first book. These are good examples of Wilder's belief in equality between husband and wife and in her independence. Many readers of the Little House books cite these qualities as a reason that Laura is a character who is a good role model for girls.

Almanzo's homestead of 320 acres was located two miles north of De Smet. Most homesteads were 160 acres, but Almanzo had filed a claim on two quarter sections. The second 160 acres was the tree claim. The government allowed two claims only if the homesteader planted 10 acres of trees. This equaled about 3,405 trees, each planted about 8 feet apart. They included cottonwoods and elms.

Laura liked the little farmhouse. It was bright and cozy, with yellow pine floors, a large pantry, and a drop-leaf table. She was also excited about the farm, and she discussed the plans in detail with Almanzo. From the beginning, Laura insisted on collaboration. She took a great interest in the homestead and felt it was important that she and Almanzo work as a team. Laura sometimes helped with the farm work, and she soon grew comfortable enough to operate the machinery and help to drive the plow. She also did all of the housework. For the first time in her life, she was in charge of taking care of the butchered hog. Laura made sausage, head cheese, and lard, just like she had watched her mother do so many times before, but she hated the stench of the hot lard and did not like the sight of the raw meat.

When they were not working, Laura and Almanzo took horseback rides around the property. Despite the hard work, they were both hopeful about the farm. They grew even happier when Laura discovered that she was going to have a baby. One spring day, on a buggy drive, they passed by a line of beautiful rose bushes, and Laura asked Almanzo what they should name the baby. He replied that they could not name the baby yet because they did not know if it was a boy or girl. Laura said, "It will be a girl and we will call her Rose." (*The First Four Years*, p. 48)

Debt quickly accumulated, and the Wilders needed to purchase horses and machinery and hire more men to help with

Although Laura Ingalls was reluctant to marry a farmer—she knew what a hard life a farmer would lead—she agreed to marriage when Almanzo Wilder proposed. The couple married in 1885. The photo above was taken shortly after the wedding.

the crops. Still, they were hopeful. The crops grew lush the first summer. Laura did the arithmetic in her head and guessed they would earn about $3,000 for the wheat, a lot of money back then. In a single day, however, their hopes were destroyed.

On an August afternoon, just before harvest, the air turned strange and still. Then suddenly the sky darkened, and hail began pounding the land. "The sunshine darkened, and the wind sighed and then fell again as it grew darker yet. Then the wind rose a little, and it grew lighter, but the light was a greenish color. Then the storm came. It rained only a little; then hailstones began to fall, at first scattering slowly, then falling thicker and faster while some of the stones were larger, some of them as large as hens' eggs." (*The First Four Years*, pp. 53–54) The hail battered and flattened the wheat, stripping the trees of leaves and branches. Although the hailstorm lasted only 20 minutes, when it was over, the wheat field was left in ruins.

Expenses grew, debts accumulated, and the baby was due in December. The Wilders still continued to hope for the best. They worked on the land, and they made plans for the next year's crops. They also decided to mortgage the homestead, which would bring them a little more money. For this to happen, however, the government required that they must live on the land, so the Wilders left the little house on the tree claim and moved into a small shanty on the homestead, a short distance away.

On December 5, 1886, Laura gave birth to a daughter, Rose. For the winter, Laura, Almanzo, and Rose stayed snug in the shanty on the prairie, but their hopes for a good crop that summer did not come true. The weather was dry, and the crop was meager. An unexplained fire burned much of the barn. Laura was worried, and she thought about giving up, but Almanzo told her they must be patient. Almanzo looked for the silver lining in clouds. This was not easy for Laura, especially when hardship struck again in the winter of 1888.

This time, Laura and Almanzo caught a life-threatening case of diphtheria. The disease was very contagious, so they sent Rose to stay with Laura's parents for a few weeks. Laura managed to recover without any lingering symptoms; however, the illness left Almanzo partially paralyzed. Although he eventually regained the use of his legs, he still sometimes struggled to walk, and he would use a cane for the rest of his life. Almanzo's hands also shook, and he no longer had the strength to do the farm work. With no other options, the Wilders decided to sell the homestead quarter and move back to the little house on the tree claim. Now, on top of everything else, they also faced medical bills. Laura felt impatient with farming life and did not think they would ever get ahead.

The next season was also disappointing. Although there was not enough rain and hot winds fanned prairie fires, the family was happy because Laura was pregnant again. She gave birth to a baby boy, but this break from hardship and sadness did not last long. Only a couple of weeks after he was born, the unnamed infant died. It was common in these days for infants to die of illnesses. Laura was grief-stricken: "To Laura, the days that followed were mercifully blurred. Her feelings were numbed and she only wanted to rest—to rest and not think." (*The First Four Years*, p. 127)

One day that same year, three-year-old Rose was helping her mother by feeding hay into the stove. Suddenly, the hay in her arms caught fire. When she dropped it, flames immediately shot up around the kitchen. Laura scrambled out of the house with Rose, but by the time Almanzo arrived from the fields, the house was burning fiercely.

Everything seemed to be conspiring against them. Although the frontier continues to be a symbol of American freedom and independence, the reality was that life in those days was extremely difficult. Over the 124-year history of the Homestead Act, more than 2 million individuals filed claims, and less than half of them actually obtained the deeds for their land. The land in the West was difficult to cultivate, and many families struggled with accumulating debts and endless poverty. Many of the movies and stories today about the American West are myths, and even Wilder's books are somewhat romantic in the way the West is portrayed. The truth is that most settlers worked themselves to exhaustion, and very few found success. The Wilders felt as though they had reached the end of the line, so they packed a covered wagon, and traveled to Minnesota, where Almanzo's father's farm was flourishing. They hoped that once they were there, they could figure out a good plan for what to do next.

Did you know...

The First Four Years was not published until after Wilder's death. The manuscript was found in 1957 among her papers on the same kind of orange school tablets she used to write the other manuscripts. Neither Rose nor Wilder herself edited it, and it is very different in style from the other Little House books. The *First Four Years* is a detailed account of the many hardships that Laura and Almanzo faced in their early years. Although it does contain interesting information about the homestead life and about their marriage, unlike the other Little House books, it does not have many moments of happiness or hopefulness. There is little dialogue, and many of the passages lack emotion. Some readers think this book is geared more for adults than for children, and they question whether Wilder intended that it be published.

The above is an illustration of a quilting party, or a "quilting bee." This kind of gathering was popular in the nineteenth century. People met in order to do some work—often a boring task—while enjoying a convivial atmosphere.

6

The Promised Land

AFTER STAYING BRIEFLY with Almanzo's parents, the Wilders decided to move to Florida, where Laura's cousin Peter was living. Although they did not know much about Florida, they hoped that the warm weather would help Almanzo recover from his illness. After the Wilders traveled by train to settle in the Florida panhandle (on the Gulf of Mexico), they were surprised to find the area to be unlike anything they had ever experienced. Laura did not like the hot, damp weather, and she also felt out of place with the people who lived there. She carried a revolver in her skirt pocket for protection. They did not adjust to this strange environment, and they headed back to South Dakota by train in less than a year.

Most of South Dakota was in a state of financial despair, and farmers faced bad crops and barren land. While the Wilders tried to figure out what they could do, they moved to a house that was close to the church and school in De Smet. Even better, it was near the home of Charles and Caroline Ingalls, who had finally given up homesteading and moved to town permanently. To earn some money, Almanzo took on carpentry and painting jobs, and Laura worked for a dressmaker. Rose often stayed with her grandparents, and she enjoyed her time with them.

Then the Wilders heard about the Ozark Mountains in Missouri. A man from De Smet who had visited the Ozarks came back with literature from the land companies. Rumors about the rich land, also known as the Land of the Big Red Apple, intrigued the Wilders. As they looked at the pictures of apple orchards, cattle, and tree-covered hills, they decided that they had nothing to lose.

It was necessary to save money for the long journey. Wilder hid a $100 bill in her special writing desk that her husband had made for her. The money would go toward the Missouri land that they planned to buy. The Wilders packed a table, chairs, iron camp stove, writing desk, and hens into the covered wagon and set out to travel with the Cooleys, a De Smet family who had two sons who were close to Rose in age.

Their trip began on July 17, 1894. In Wilder's journal, which was published many years later as *On the Way Home,* she closely observed the setting and the weather. On the long and exhausting journey, they averaged

20 miles a day, pushing through harsh winds and a heat wave. The temperature was often 90 degrees; sometimes it was more than 100 degrees. The first part of the trip, through Kansas and Nebraska, was the most difficult. It was hot and dusty, and as they crossed the plains, the wind blew fiercely over the dry land. Wilder wrote in her journal, "The more I see of Nebraska the less I like it." (*On the Way Home*, p. 35)

The Wilders and the Cooleys were certainly not the only settlers in search of better lands. A migration across America was in progress, and the group encountered many others who were looking for rich land and good crops along the way. Everyone seemed tired and travel-weary.

Did you know...

Several films based on the Little House series have been produced for television. In 2000, *Beyond the Prairie: The True Story of Laura Ingalls Wilder* aired on television, and Part II aired in 2002. Produced by Marcus Cole, these two movies focused on the final four books in the series, from *The Long Winter* to *The First Four Years*. In 2005, a five-episode miniseries called *Laura Ingalls Wilder's Little House on the Prairie* aired on television as part of *The Wonderful World of Disney* series. This miniseries focused on the two early books, *Little House in the Big Woods* and *Little House on the Prairie*.

Many immigrants came to the American Midwest; these included Canadians, Swedes, and Germans. The Wilders also met German and Russian Mennonites.

Six weeks later, after 650 miles of travel, the Wilders reached the Ozarks. Wilder immediately felt hopeful, and on August 25, she wrote, "Well, we are in the Ozarks at last, just in the beginning of them, and they are beautiful." (*On the Way Home*, p. 73) The Ozark Mountains are located in the southern half of Missouri and northwest Arkansas. The landscape is not extremely mountainous, but it is a plateau that is split up with rolling hills and chiseled valleys, with many streams running down from the hills.

Everything was green, and wild fruit trees with blackberries, cherries, plums, peaches, and persimmons grew all along the roadside. "It is a drowsy country that makes you feel wide awake and alive but somehow contented," observed Wilder. (*On the Way Home*, p. 78) Instead of flat plains, the land rolled with hills, and the wind was gentle and peaceful. Laura immediately saw the potential for such land.

The Wilders stopped in Mansfield, the crossroads and the highest point of the Ozarks. They camped in the woods and began to search for land to buy. Although they looked at many farms, they did not find anything that was right. One day, Almanzo came back with news that he had found a place. Years later, Rose recalled the happiness of this day, "When he was excited my father always held himself quiet and steady, moving and speaking with deliberation. Sometimes my quick mother flew out at him, but this day she was soft and warm." (*On the Way Home*, p. 88)

There was a temporary panic when Laura opened the desk drawer and discovered that the $100 bill was missing. "There was a shock, like stepping in the dark on a top step that isn't there," recalled Rose. (*On the Way Home*, p. 91) She also remembered that her mother had asked whether she had touched the money, or played with it, and seven-year-old Rose felt indignant and angry. Miraculously, they found the money: It had slipped into a crack in the desk.

The Wilders purchased the land on September 24, 1894. It had been left in a state of neglect. Nothing was cultivated, and the ground was rocky and hard. There was a thick forest on the land that would need to be cleared for fields, and the log cabin on the hill was weathered and without windows. Four hundred apple seedlings were waiting to be planted. The previous owners had ordered the apple trees from a nursery, but once they realized how much work farming would be, they abandoned the seedlings and the farm.

Despite the problems, Wilder could see promising possibilities: They already had a cabin, a spring, and future crops. Mansfield was only about a mile away, so it would be easy for Rose to get to school. Called the Gem City of the Ozarks, Mansfield had a new railroad line and mining activity that created jobs. New businesses appeared, including a bakery, a general store, a drugstore, and a bank. There was even an opera house!

Wilder named their new home Rocky Ridge Farm. She quickly made the little cabin snug, and Almanzo began to cut down trees to clear the land. The trees would also be used for winter fuel. In addition to the tremendous amount of housework she had to do, Wilder spent a great deal of

When the Wilders moved to Mansfield, Missouri, they purchased farmland that they named Rocky Ridge. It was close to a good school, which their daughter, Rose, attended. Laura and Almanzo gave Rose (above) a donkey so that she could ride to school.

time helping her husband with the farm. Small, quick, and strong, her energy seemed endless. She helped Almanzo use a two-man crosscut saw, and they worked together in the woods, clearing the trees. Wilder felt hopeful for the first time in years.

Meanwhile, Rose attended school on the east edge of town. She was very intelligent and precocious, and, like her mother, she loved to read and to spell. At night, the small family gathered and read aloud, just as Wilder's parents had done. Laura would read aloud Tennyson's poems, along with adventurous stories and novels, such as *Conquest of Mexico, Conquest of Peru, The Green Mountain Boys, The Leatherstocking Tales,* and *The House of the Seven Gables.* They also liked reading the serial stories in newspapers, which were popular with settlers in the nineteenth century. Each week, a new chapter appeared. They always ended abruptly, so readers would want more.

Although the work on the farm took up most of their time and energy, the Wilders also found time to socialize. They visited the Cooleys and other families, and they attended dances, quilting bees, outdoor singings, and church picnics. One of the easiest ways for settlers to socialize with each other was through the church. Since there was no Congregational church in Mansfield, the Wilders went to the Methodist church. In their free time, the Wilders still liked to go horseback riding, and they even gave Rose a donkey to ride to school. It was named Spookendyke. Rose later wrote how the stubborn donkey would suddenly slump his neck and shoulders when going down a hill, forcing her to tumble off over its head. Spookendyke also liked to stand outside the school, where it was tied up while she was in class, and bray loudly, which embarrassed Rose.

Slowly, the stony Ozark soil began to produce. The Wilders added peach and pear trees to the orchards, and they decided that it would make the most sense if they each focused on a specialty. Laura would be in charge of poultry and would sell chickens and eggs, and Almanzo would handle the cows. They bought more land to expand the farm, and they added windows to the cabin.

The apple trees would take seven years to bear fruit, and it would take a few years before the farm would be self-supporting. Their finances were still in trouble. Almanzo, whose health was still not good, was exhausted from trying to clear the trees and stones from the land. The Wilders knew that they needed to bring in a more steady income, so they decided to rent a house just on the edge of town.

For a while, Almanzo took a job as a drayman, in which he met trains at the depot and unloaded shipments of merchandise for the stores. Laura and Rose were always the first to know when new styles or new bolts of fabric arrived. Almanzo also worked for years selling kerosene for an oil company, and Laura served hot meals as a way to earn extra money. The townsfolk were happy to get the Wilders' farm-fresh eggs, new milk, fruits, and vegetables.

Although the Wilders had to spend much of their time in town and work the farm from a distance, they felt hopeful about their future. Laura enjoyed the farming life. She felt connected to the land and expressed a strong interest in running a small-scale farm. Farming was her main interest, and she did not think about writing. At this point in her life, she had only written school compositions, teenaged poetry, letters to family, and a journal documenting their trip. She was a mother, a farmer's wife, and a homemaker. What would be her path to one day becoming a famous children's book author?

Above, the entire Ingalls family poses together (from left): Caroline, Carrie, Laura, Charles, Grace, and Mary. Although Laura Ingalls Wilder lived far from her family in later life, she kept in close touch with them.

7

From Farming to Writing

WILDER RECEIVED OCCASIONAL news from her family in De Smet, which described what was going on in town. Charles and Caroline were happy in their house in town on Third Street. Mary and Carrie still lived at home with them. Mary read Braille books, played music, and stayed busy with her handwork. Carrie worked at the *De Smet News and Leader* office. Grace, their youngest daughter, had been a school-teacher and was now married to a farmer.

Then, in May 1902, Laura Wilder received word from De Smet that her father was very ill. She immediately took a train to South Dakota. She made it in time to see her father and to say good-bye to him. Charles Ingalls died at age 66, with Caroline and his four daughters around him. Wilder had always been very close to her father, and it was a difficult loss. She took comfort in knowing that her father had led a full and adventurous life and was loved very much.

Wilder said good-bye to her mother and to her sisters. It was the last time that she would see her mother and Mary. It was difficult then for families and friends who lived far from each to visit very often. Wilder returned to her home in Mansfield to her husband and daughter.

Rose was a very bright child who read constantly, and she checked out many books from the school library. Once, a family who owned a tremendous number of books moved into town, and Rose borrowed them all, including *The Decline and Fall of the Roman Empire.* In Mansfield, locally-available education extended only to the eighth grade. Because Rose craved more intellectual stimulation, she wanted to continue school beyond this level. Almanzo's sister Eliza offered to let Rose live with her in Louisiana so she could enroll in the high school there. For a year, Rose lived away from home and learned as much as she could, including four years of Latin that she crammed into one year.

Rose was an ambitious girl who wanted more than Mansfield could offer. She did not like the isolation of the small town, and she wanted to see more of the world. When she was 17 years old, she left home to work as a telegraph operator in Kansas City, Missouri, earning $2.50 a week. It was unusual for a 17-year-old girl to leave home, but the Wilders realized that Rose was different from the other Mansfield girls, and they supported her decision. Women still had very few opportunities, but it was the turn of the century, and there were more possibilities than ever before. Rose was part of the movement of the working girls, who were considered to be very modern and cosmopolitan. In Kansas City, Rose shortened her skirts and cut her long hair. These fashionable styles created a stir on her visits back to Mansfield.

The Wilders lived in town and worked the farm from a distance for more than a decade. After they inherited $500 from Almanzo's parents, they sold the town house and returned to Rocky Ridge to finish building the farmhouse. Laura had been dreaming about the farmhouse for a long time. She knew how she wanted it to look, and she drew plans for Almanzo of a 10-room farmhouse, which included 4 porches, a rock fireplace, and a library. One important part, in her eyes, was the rock fireplace. There was timber and rock all around the property, and they hired men to help build the house. Almanzo, who was worn out from hauling rock, told Laura they would have to use brick for the fireplace. She objected, argued, and wept, until she finally convinced Almanzo to build the fireplace from rocks.

When the house was finished, in 1913, Laura was happy. Visitors were often surprised by the design, and they commented on how unique the house was. It was very different from the traditional farmhouses in the area. Although it was an unusual house, it seemed perfect for the Wilders.

For the first time, the Wilders now had a flourishing farm. When they had first moved in, nothing grew on the land, and they were almost penniless. Now, although they still had very little money, their farming business was more stable. They had learned hard lessons in South Dakota not to rely on only one crop. Now they grew apples, pears, peaches, corn, wheat, strawberries, and raspberries. Laura canned and preserved the fruits and vegetables, churned butter, and baked bread. Almanzo took care of a herd of white Jersey cows, and Laura found success in the poultry business, tending a flock of Leghorn hens. She designed a henhouse that was clean and airy, and her goal was to make a dollar profit per hen over the hen's lifetime.

Wilder had a good head for business. She liked farming and was interested in the different aspects of it. As her poultry business began to gain recognition around the Ozarks, she was invited to speak at farmers' meetings, to share her ideas and methods about the business of raising chickens. One day, she was too busy to attend a meeting where she was scheduled to give a talk, so she sent a speech to be read in her absence. It was a good thing that she did not show up, because her absence would change her life in ways that she had never dreamed.

Someone at the meeting read Wilder's speech, and it very much impressed John Case, the editor of a farm weekly called *The Missouri Ruralist*. He asked Wilder to submit articles for the paper. This was the very start of Wilder's writing career; she was 44 years old.

Wilder's first article, "Favors the Small Farm," with the byline "Mrs. A.J. Wilder," appeared in February 1911. Wilder had always liked to write compositions in school, but she had never thought about becoming a writer. Although she continued to farm, garden, and do housework, now Wilder also turned her attention to writing essays, poems, and articles for the *Ruralist*. She interviewed her neighbors and various country people, and she conducted research for articles. Wilder's basic message was that country life was good. She praised the rural way of life and small-scale farming, and the most common themes in her columns were hard work, helping others, and independence.

In the beginning, Wilder's articles appeared only occasionally, but her work eventually became a steady feature. She wrote a column called "The Farm Home," and later,

"As a Farm Woman Thinks." Writing often about Rocky Ridge Farm, she encouraged women to be active partners with their husbands. Wilder became known as an expert on farm life. She also wrote a few articles for the *St. Louis Post-Dispatch* and the *Kansas City Star*. Although she was not paid much, she enjoyed the work.

Wilder was not the only writer in the family: Rose was now a successful journalist. In fact, Rose would become a somewhat well-known writer, years before anyone had ever heard of her mother.

Rose lived a much different life than most Mansfield women: she traveled around the world and socialized with writers and artists. With her successful career and independent lifestyle, she would have been considered a "New Woman," which was a feminist ideal in the early twentieth century. As a Western Union telegrapher, Rose had traveled widely, and she started writing for the *Kansas City Post* while living in Kansas City. Then, Rose settled in San Francisco with her husband, Gillette Lane. For a while, Rose worked as a real estate agent. She was one of the first female agents in northern California. Next, she wrote the women's page for the *San Francisco Bulletin*. By 1915, at age 29, Rose had established herself as a journalist. During her career, she interviewed entrepreneur Henry Ford and actor Charlie Chaplin.

Wilder exchanged letters about writing with Rose. She was proud of Rose's accomplishments and ambition, and she was impressed with her life in San Francisco. Rose wanted her mother, whom she called Mama Bess, to visit the city. She thought that it would inspire her to write: "I think by getting away from it all for a while, and playing around with a bunch of people who are writing and drawing and otherwise being near-artists, you will get an entirely new viewpoint on things there, and be able to see a lot of new things to write when you go back." (*West From Home*, p. 5)

In 1915, Laura Wilder boarded a train bound for the West Coast. Almanzo stayed behind to look after the farm. Although Wilder loved her home in the Ozarks, she also

Did you know...

Laura Ingalls Wilder's daughter Rose Wilder Lane was a novelist, journalist, and political theorist. Her two most successful novels were *Let the Hurricane Roar* (1932), which is now better known as *Young Pioneers*, and *Free Land* (1938). She was also the author of *Old Home Town* (1935), a fictionalized account of her own experiences in Mansfield, Missouri, and several other books. Rose also found success as a ghost writer, someone who writes books for other people, such as her book on Herbert Hoover. In her later years, Rose wrote about her philosophies of personal freedom and liberty. She became one of the more influential American libertarians of the middle twentieth century. Libertarians believe that individuals should be free to do whatever they wish with their person or property, as long as they do not infringe on the same liberty of others. Rose was the adoptive grandmother and mentor of Roger MacBride, the Libertarian Party's 1976 candidate for President of the United States.

liked to travel. Like her father, she had a somewhat adventurous, restless spirit.

Wilder watched the changing landscape through the train window, and on the journey, she wrote letters to Almanzo, describing everything that she saw. These letters were published as the book, *West From Home,* after her death. At first, Wilder was unimpressed with the flat western landscape. She wrote, "So far everything out of the car window has been ugly since I left the Ozarks." (*West From Home*, p. 15)

As the train moved closer to the West Coast, however, she no longer felt this way. Like her fiction, Wilder's letters are filled with description and vivid imagery. In one letter, she wrote, "I saw the sun rise on the desert as I lay in my berth and it was lovely. The bare, perfectly bare, rocky mountains in all kinds of heaps and piles as though the winds had drifted into heaps and they had turned to rock, were purple in the hollows and rose and gold and pink on the lighter places." (*West From Home*, p. 24)

Rose lived on Russian Hill, a haven for writers, artists, and architects. Wilder loved the neighborhood, as well as the entire city of San Francisco. In a letter home, she wrote, "You know I have never cared for cities but San Francisco is simply the most beautiful thing." (*West From Home*, p. 35) She met Rose's artist and writer friends, and she and Rose took long rambling walks around the city and rode in the new streetcars. Wilder also attended the 1915 World's Fair, which was held to celebrate the completion of the Panama Canal. There was a sense of adventure and progress in the air.

At the fair, there was food from all over the world, and Wilder tasted dishes that she had never heard of before.

*Above, Rose Wilder poses for a photograph taken in Europe in the
1920s. Rose was an unusual woman for her time; she left home at
age 17 and traveled widely, often on her own.*

This inspired her to write an article for *The Ruralist*. She praised the international cuisine and encouraged her Missouri farming friends to try new dishes. She even passed on a few of the recipes, including "Mexican Tamale Loaf," "Chinese Almond Cakes," and "Italian White Tagliarini."

In her letters to Almanzo, Wilder described the city of San Francisco, as well how she and Rose spent their time. She also asked questions about the farm and seemed concerned about growing debts and finances, although there was nothing in these letters to indicate that Wilder was thinking about embarking on a writing career. Rose was correct, however, when she said that this trip would be good for her mother. Wilder spent two months in San Francisco with Rose, and when she returned to her beloved hills of Missouri, she felt renewed and turned again to farming and writing.

Above, Laura Ingalls Wilder signs books for children in the 1950s. Though Wilder worked hard all her life on farms and as a teacher, she also had a gift for writing, which emerged in the publication of her Little House books.

8

A Children's Book Author Is Born

WILDER TURNED 50 the year the United States entered World War I, which was fought mostly in Europe. More than 9 million solders died on its battlefields, and millions of civilians were also killed. Wilder supported President Woodrow Wilson's decision to enter the war on April 6, 1917, after he had maintained a policy of neutrality during its first years.

Wilder began to work for the Mansfield Farm Loan Association as secretary-treasurer, a position she held for 10 years. The Farm Loan Association allowed farmers to borrow money or buy and improve land through the Federal Land Bank in St.

Louis. Wilder was very good at her job, and she liked help-ing farmers. She worked from an office in her farmhouse.

Farming was Wilder's main interest, but she was also active in the Mansfield community. She worked to establish social events for country women, who were often isolated from each other. The group she created, the Athenians, provided educational experiences and friendships among members. One of its goals was to create a county library. By now, the Wilders were financially comfortable. Most of the women Wilder spent time with were the wives of business owners, doctors, and lawyers.

While living in San Francisco, in 1918, Rose had divorced Gillette Lane. She was now completely inde-pendent and took on more writing jobs. Rose published a nonfiction book about Henry Ford, and she wrote her first novel, called *Diverging Roads*. Whenever she visited her parents in Mansfield, the newspaper called her a "writer of great note," and people in the town were thrilled to talk to her. She brought a sense of excitement and worldliness to the small town. Rose lived for a while in Greenwich Village, New York City, and then in 1920, she sailed to Europe, where she traveled to France, Budapest, Athens, London, Vienna, Prague, and Albania, a Balkan country in southeastern Europe. Albania was one of Rose's favorite places in the world.

After several years of travel, Rose sailed back to the United States and arrived home in time for Christmas in 1923. Her parents were delighted to see her, and there were many parties in town to welcome her. Until Wilder published the Little House books, Rose was the most famous person to come from Mansfield. Rose set up her typewriter in the farmhouse, and she turned her attention to writing articles and short stories. Laura and Almanzo were happy to have her in the house. By then, Rose was making a fairly good income, and she often helped out her parents. Although the farm was productive, it was still a difficult business, and there always seemed to be more debts and bills. Rose gave her parents $500 a year to help with the many expenses on Rocky Ridge. Another one of her gifts to her parents was a blue 1923 Buick, shipped from New York. Mansfield was filled with anticipation and excitement the day it arrived. Rose taught both of her parents to drive, but Laura usually let Almanzo get behind the wheel. The Wilders named their new car Isabelle.

Rose's presence on the farm influenced Wilder's own desire to write. After working at the Farm Loan Association for 10 years, Wilder resigned from her job and focused more on her writing. She wanted to branch out from her columns for *The Ruralist*, so Rose helped her mother with several articles that were published in *McCall's* and *Country Gentleman*. Rose urged her mother to write more regularly and to send her work to high-paying, high-profile magazines instead of *The Ruralist*, which only paid $5 to $10 per story.

A restless spirit, Rose left again to live in Albania, but she came back home after two years. She saw that her parents were growing older and more fragile, and she wanted to help them. At this point, Almanzo was 71 years old, and Laura was 60. Rose felt that the farm work was too much for her parents to handle, and she encouraged them to hire someone to do most of the work. When Rose sold her fictitious serial about the Ozarks, called "Cindy," to *The Country Gentleman* for $10,000, she decided to use the money to build a new, more modern, house for her parents.

The new house, just across the ridge from the old house, was an English-style five-room cottage, also called the Rock House. It was modern and unusual. After her parents moved into the new house, Rose had the old farmhouse wired with electricity. This became her new home. Now she could write here, with privacy, but still be close to her parents. One of her friends also came to stay on Rocky Ridge for a while. Cheery Helen Boylston, a war nurse Rose had met in Poland, was interested in being a writer. Her nickname was "Troub," because she always seemed to attract trouble. Instead of writing, she spent most of her time horseback riding.

Then, in October 1929, the stock market crashed, which marked the beginning of the Great Depression. People who lived in urban areas suffered greatly, and long lines formed at soup kitchens, in bread lines, and at employment agencies. Many people lost their jobs and homes. In rural areas, farmers who had suffered when prices for crops fell in the early 1920s continued to experience financial hardship.

Wilder worried about the effects of this on her family. By now, the farm was paid off and their finances were mostly stable, but unfortunately, the Wilders had invested in the stock market. Much of their savings was wiped out, and they had to depend on Rose, who now needed to earn more money from her writing.

Wilder looked around her and saw how the much the world had changed since her childhood days on the prairie. The 1920s had brought great advancements to society in the fields of science, technology, and politics. The women's suffrage movement made gigantic strides, and in 1920, women in the United States were granted the right to vote. The television was invented, and the first all-color, all-talking movie was produced in 1929. Prohibition was in full force. In Europe, Hitler published *Mein Kampf,* a book that foreshadowed the rise of fascism and many of the events of the 1930s.

The frontier that Wilder's family had traveled to was now completely gone. There was no more untouched land in America, and the pioneer and settler ways of life were quickly disappearing. Wilder wanted to preserve some of those memories that she felt were an important part of American history. Over the past few years, Wilder had been

Did you know...

There are many Web sites and publications for fans of Laura Ingalls Wilder and the Little House series. For example, the HarperCollins Web site, "Come Home to Little House," at http://www. littlehousebooks.com/index.html, lists all of the Little House books and the spin-off series, along with trivia and recipes. There is also an e-zine called *The Homesteader* about Wilder; it appears twice a year. The Web site, http://www .homesteadernewsletter.com says the publication is "created by Laura fans, for Laura fans." There is also a special site for kids called "Laura Ingalls Wilder, Frontier Girl," at http://webpages .marshall.edu/~irby1/laura/frames.html. This Web site provides much information about Wilder's life. You can also listen to the songs played on Pa's fiddle and see pictures of the places the Ingalls and Wilder families lived. These are just a few examples of the many Web sites and home pages dedicated to Laura Ingalls Wilder.

exploring how she could use the memories and material from her childhood as a basis for articles in the *Ruralist*. Now those columns did not seem big enough for everything she wanted to say.

Wilder wanted to tell the story of her childhood. She felt the experiences were important for people to read about, and they were stories that needed to be told. She also wanted to memorialize the memories of her family, and to share with people the history of an America that no longer existed. Wilder decided to write her autobiography, and she also hoped it would bring in a little income.

Writing with a pencil in a cheap blue-lined school tablet, Wilder began with her family's journey to Kansas. She wrote the story of her life until her marriage, and then she stopped. She called the book *Pioneer Girl*. When she finished, she passed the handwritten manuscript over to Rose, who typed up the pages and gave her mother suggestions to improve the story. Of all of Wilder's books, this first one received the lightest editing by Rose.

In recent years, controversy has emerged about what role Rose played in writing the Little House books. Some people argue that Wilder only relied on Rose for connections to literary agents and publishers; others say that Rose basically wrote the books. Realistically, the truth probably lies somewhere in between. Wilder wrote the books, but she relied on Rose to edit them. The two most likely collaborated on them. Wilder was a compelling storyteller, and Rose was a skilled writer. Both mother and daughter were ambitious and determined, and it was a working partnership that seemed to serve them both.

Rose sent her mother's manuscript to her agent in New York. The agent liked the story and sent it to several New York publishers. A few people expressed interest in the

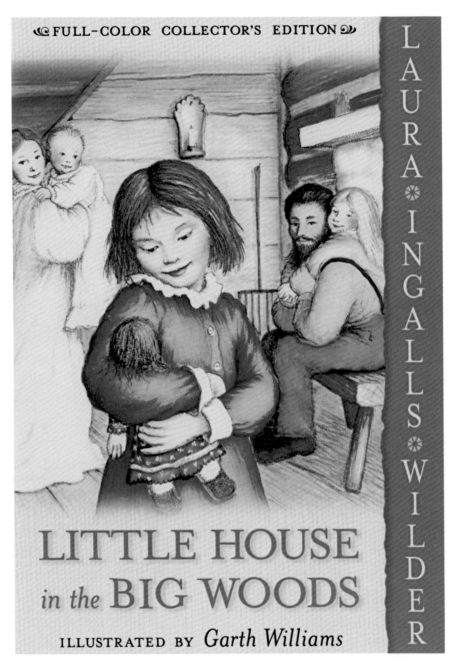

ᴥFULL-COLOR COLLECTOR'S EDITIONᴥ

LAURA ✳ INGALLS ✳ WILDER

LITTLE HOUSE
in the BIG WOODS

ILLUSTRATED BY *Garth Williams*

Little House in the Big Woods *was the first book that Laura Ingalls Wilder wrote. It tells the stories of her life in the Big Woods with Ma, Pa, and Mary. The book was published in 1932. The profits helped support her and Almanzo throughout the Great Depression.*

story, but no one wanted to buy it. Just when it seemed as though nothing would happen with it, the editor of the children's section of Harper & Brothers read it and loved it. Harper & Brothers agreed to publish it, but only with major changes. They asked Wilder to rewrite and restructure it.

Rose helped her mother with the structure of the book, suggesting that she concentrate on one part instead of covering such a big expanse of time. Then Wilder rewrote the book, focusing on her memories of living in the Big Woods with Pa, Ma, and Mary. She included many of her father's stories, and she also included details about butchering hogs and making bullets. These were things that she had grown up with, but that by this time most children did not know about. She called this book *Little House in the Big Woods.*

After Wilder finished the manuscript, she and Almanzo took a trip to South Dakota. They went in the Buick, going the same route they had traveled to Missouri by wagon 37 years earlier. Just like the first time, the trip was hot and dusty. When they arrived in De Smet, they found a different place. It was now a modern little town. The trip was bittersweet. They drove to their old homestead, the land that had given them so much trouble. There were no buildings left on their tree claim. It was a thing of the past. On the way home, they visited Carrie and Grace. Carrie lived near De Smet, and Grace, who had married a Black Hills mine owner, lived near the foot of Mount Rushmore. Wilder's mother had died in 1924, and her sister Mary had died in 1928.

Little House in the Big Woods was published in 1932. Wilder liked the pen and ink drawings by Helen Sewell, and she was thrilled to see her own words in print. The Junior Literary Guild picked the book for its 1932 selection, and soon libraries and schools all around the country were praising Wilder's writing. The novel received many glowing reviews. The *New York Times* felt that the characters were "very much alive" and "the portrait of Laura's father, especially, is drawn with loving care and reality."[4] Reviewers praised the simple style, charming characters, and pleasurable voice.

The publication of *Little House in the Big Woods* changed Wilder's life. At 65 years old, she was no longer Laura Wilder, Bessie Wilder, or Mrs. A.J. Wilder: Now she was known as Laura Ingalls Wilder. The readers who enjoyed the first book would eventually number in the millions. Children fell in love with the books, as did teachers and librarians. Wilder was very happy, and she wanted to keep writing. She had much more to say.

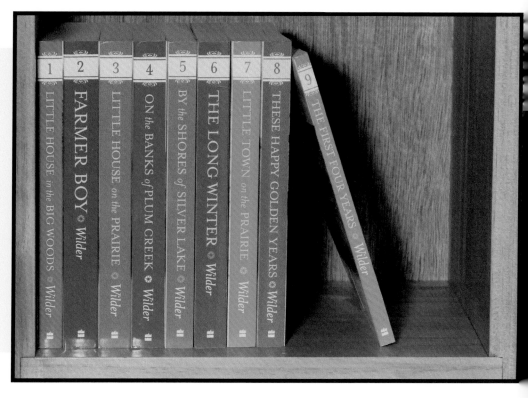

There are nine books in the full Little House series, chronicling Laura Ingalls Wilder's life, from early childhood to the first years of her marriage, plus some stories from Almanzo Wilder's boyhood in the book Farmer Boy.

9

Fame in the Golden Years

WILDER WROTE BOOKS for about a dozen years. During that time, she achieved more success than most writers do over a lifetime. After *Little House in the Big Woods* was published, children began to write letters, asking to read more. Harper & Brothers also asked for a second book. This time, Wilder decided to write Almanzo's story.

Wilder wanted her book to be about Almanzo's boyhood in Malone, New York. Although she knew some of the story, she needed him to talk about specific memories. Almanzo was a very private and quiet person, and it was not easy to get him to talk freely about the past. Wilder persisted until she finally had enough material to write *Farmer Boy*, which was published in 1933. *Farmer Boy* also received good reviews, although it did not receive as much publicity as her first book. When the mail came now, there were letters for Almanzo, in addition to the usual fan letters for Wilder.

Before *Farmer Boy* hit the press, Wilder was already at work on another volume about her own childhood. She had realized with the first book just how many stories she had inside of her, and how many childhood memories and family stories that she wanted to tell. Now she turned her attention to the story about her family's life on the Osage Indian Reservation in Kansas. Wilder's mind was filled with memories, and she wrote down everything she could remember. Writing in pencil in the blue-lined school tablets as before, she described the prairie setting and the characters of her family, making all of it very realistic.

This third book was *Little House on the Prairie,* published in 1935. Although Wilder had written three books, there were more memories to explore and more stories to tell. She came up with a plan: She decided she would continue to write about her childhood, and that she would do this in a series of books.

On the Banks of Plum Creek, the next book in the series, was named a Newbery Honor Book, an award given to the most outstanding children's book of the year. This book brought the reader to Walnut Grove, which became the famous setting for the television show 40 years later. When Wilder finished her fourth book, she was 70 years old.

Wilder continued to go to Rose for help with editing and revising. Rose asked her mother many questions, jogging her memory about things she may have forgotten. Wilder remembered the Owens family and the little sod house.

She drew maps of Plum Creek, and this helped her remember the way everything had looked. She also conducted research on the time period and setting. Although Wilder wrote the Little House books based on personal memories and family stories, she wanted her books to be accurate in their historical detail.

Because they lived right across from each other, it was easy for Laura to go to Rose for help. But then Rose was offered a contract to write a volume about Missouri's history and politics, and she moved to Columbia to do historical research for the book at the University of Missouri. When she left, she had just finished a collection of short stories set in a fictionalized Mansfield setting called *Old Home Town*. Rose would not return to Rocky Ridge for many years.

After Rose left, the Wilders moved out of the English-style cabin and back into their old farmhouse. Although they appreciated Rose's help in building them a smaller, more manageable house, they had never felt quite at home there. They missed the farmhouse that they had designed and built themselves. They were both very happy about the way their farm had blossomed over the years. What began as a 40-acre farm of rough land had eventually turned into 200 acres, and it was now a relatively prosperous poultry, dairy, and fruit farm. Rocky Ridge was a beautiful place, with cleared fields, fruit trees, and shady trees.

Although Wilder now devoted much of her time to writing, she also continued with her farming routines. She still cooked and took care of the house, while Almanzo tended his goats, worked in the woodshop, and gardened. Over the years, the Wilders made various road trips. They lived a quiet, modest lifestyle, even as Wilder's books caused ripples of excitement around the country.

The house on Rocky Ridge Farm (above), was Wilder's favorite place. She and Almanzo lived out their years there, with their daughter Rose visiting or even living on the property at different times.

Children loved her books. Wilder made learning about pioneer life entertaining and fun. The children felt more connected to her books because Wilder chose to show almost everything through Laura's eyes. They wrote many letters, begging for more stories about the Ingalls family and asking questions about the characters. Fans were surprised and excited when Wilder showed up at a book fair in

Detroit, Michigan. They crowded in to hear her speak and to get her autograph.

The Little House books continued to receive awards and glowing reviews. By the mid-1930s, the royalties from the books brought a steady and sizable income to the Wilders for the first time in their marriage. The next book in the series was *By the Shores of Silver Lake*, which took longer to write than the other manuscripts. *By the Shores of Silver Lake* was also chosen as a Newbery Honor book, with the *New Yorker* calling the book "touching, unsentimental, and real Americana."[5]

After Wilder sent off the book to her publishers, she felt as though she needed a break. Still adventurous, she went on a road trip with Almanzo, and their younger friends, Silas and Neta Seal. They took Route 66 across Oklahoma, Texas, New Mexico, Arizona, and California, then they went up to Oregon and Washington. The Wilders and Seals went to Idaho and Wyoming, and then on their way back, they stopped at the Wilder's old home in South Dakota to visit Laura's sister Carrie and to see old friends in De Smet. Part of reason for the trip was that Wilder wanted to do research for her Little House books. She took notes on what she saw, and she refreshed her memory about the years that she lived here.

In 1940, Wilder published *The Long Winter*, about her family's first year in De Smet, when blizzards whirled over the town. She originally called the book "The Hard Winter," but the editors at Harpers & Brothers thought the title sounded too negative for children.

Next, Wilder worked on the seventh book in the series, *Little Town on the Prairie*, about the development of De Smet. This book was also named as a Newbery Honor

Book. At this point in her writing career, Wilder's books had sold thousands of copies. She now made more money from her books than she ever had on the farm.

Although the Wilders continued to live quiet lives, they were not like the other Mansfield residents. Laura Ingalls Wilder was a famous writer. Her mailbox was always stuffed with fan letters, cards, and gifts from children, librarians, and teachers. She felt grateful to her loyal fans, and she appreciated their support. Readers eagerly awaited the next book in the series, and Wilder continued to deliver. She also answered all of the children's letters, telling her editor, "You would be astonished at the number of letters. I answer them for I cannot bear to disappoint children."[6] Sometimes children, teachers, and librarians stopped by, and the Wilders showed them around the farm.

The Wilders were still happy to be living on Rocky Ridge Farm, although they missed Rose, who now lived on the other side of the country. For a while, Rose had lived in New York City, where she worked on stories about pioneers. She asked her mother and father many questions about the pioneer days, and they shared their memories with her. Then she wrote a novel called *Free Land*, which was published as a serial in eight parts in the *Saturday Evening Post*. This best-selling novel received many favorable reviews, and Rose was paid about $30,000, which in today's dollars would be nearly $400,000. Rose was now 51 years old, and this was her last major work of fiction. After living in New York, Rose moved to Danbury, Connecticut, where she lived for the rest of her life. The Wilders stayed in touch with her as much as they could. They wrote letters, and were still very much a part of each other's lives, bonding over politics and thoughts about economics.

Wilder witnessed many monumental events in the world over her lifetime. One of those monumental events was World War II, which started in 1939 and ended in 1945. It was the largest armed conflict the world has ever seen, with

Did you know...

The Little House books are also popular in Japan. *The Long Winter* was published in Japan, in 1949, under the Japanese title *Nagai Fuyu*. After World War II, during the American occupation of Japan, a number of American books were translated and published in Japan with the goal of "teaching the American way of life." All publishing materials were strictly examined, censored, and revised by General Headquarters, with General Douglas MacArthur as Supreme Commander for the Allied Powers. MacArthur recommended *The Long Winter*, and it was the first to be granted permission for translation and publication. The Japanese Library Association and the Association of Scholars of Children's Literature listed *The Long Winter* in the children's choices, and it was widely distributed to libraries and schools. The popularity of Wilder's novel surpassed the popularity of other American books, including *The Good Earth*, *Little Women*, and *Gone With the Wind*. Wilder's books are still printed and read in Japan. In 1975, a Japanese animated version of the Little House series was released under the title *Sōgen no shōjō Laura*, which means *Laura the Prairie Girl*. It ran 26 episodes, about 24 minutes each.

air, land, and sea battles. The United States entered the war on December 7, 1941, after Pearl Harbor was bombed. By the time the war ended, the world had experienced much devastation; people were stunned by the revelation of the Nazi concentration camps, as well as by the annihilation of the atomic bombs.

Despite the horrors of the war overseas, Wilder's books about the prairie life continued to touch young readers. Her books took her audience to a different place; the idea of the frontier captivated people. It seemed like a simpler way of life, although in truth, life during those years was not at all easy.

When Wilder was 76 years old, she finished the last book in the series, *These Happy Golden Years,* another Newbery Honor Book. Wilder felt she had reached the end of the series, and she announced that she would stop writing. Her publishers and fans were disappointed that they would not hear any more of her stories.

Wilder had written the Little House series in 11 years, and now she felt ready to retire. She wanted to spend the rest of her days quietly with Almanzo. They worked around the house and gardened, took care of their goats, went on drives together, and, in the evening, played cribbage and read.

Meanwhile, Wilder's books were selling so well in the United States that Harper & Brothers decided to publish new editions, with new illustrations by Garth Williams, a prominent American illustrator who was known for his work on children's books. Williams had also illustrated E.B. White's *Charlotte's Web*, and several Little Golden Books.

The Wilders were too old to do any more farming, but they did not want to leave Rocky Ridge, so in 1948, they sold the farm to a young couple, Harland and Gireda Shorter. The Shorters lived in the house that Rose had built. Part of the arrangement was that the Wilders would be able to spend the rest of their days in the old farmhouse. Thanks to the income from the Little House books, they now lived without any financial worries.

Wilder still felt healthy, but Almanzo was growing weaker. Ever since his bout with diphtheria 60 years previously, he had moved slowly, relying on a cane. Now he was 92 years old. Although he moved even more slowly and shakily, he still enjoyed his favorite activities, such as woodworking and gardening. Almanzo was known in Mansfield as a quiet, gentle, hardworking man. Then, in July, Almanzo suffered a serious heart attack. Although his health improved, he had a second heart attack on October 23, 1949, and he died at home.

After 64 years of married life, Wilder was now alone, and she missed Almanzo deeply. She had many people who cared about her and gave her the support she needed. Her friends helped her through those first days after Almanzo's death, and Rose arrived from Connecticut to be with her mother. It was Rose's first time on the farm in a dozen years.

Wilder was lonely in the big house, but she was happy there and decided to stay on the farm. She loved the land, and did not want to leave. Although she was no longer writing, Wilder continued to demonstrate her independence and strength until the end of her life. She spent her time reading, sewing, and listening to the radio. She did not own a television.

Neighbors and Wilder's circle of friends looked in on her, and once a week, she went into town. Wilder enjoyed these trips; she always dressed up, and had someone drive her. In town, she shopped for groceries and other necessities, and then she stopped by the library to pick up her weekly reading. Aware that Wilder enjoyed mysteries and westerns, the librarian faithfully set aside the new ones for her. She especially liked the western writer Zane Gray.

In the last stage of her life, Wilder was showered with awards and honors. The Detroit Public Library opened a new branch library and named it for Laura Ingalls Wilder. It was the first library in the city to be named for a living person and for a woman. A library in Pomona, California, dedicated the children's department of the library as the Laura Ingalls Wilder Room. Then, in 1951, Mansfield named the local library after Wilder.

A dedication ceremony was held at the Mansfield High School gymnasium. Wilder was 84 years old. She wore her favorite red velvet dress, and she presented the library with autographed copies of her books, as well as souvenirs and gifts from fans. She also donated the trowel that had been used to build the Wilder's home at Rocky Ridge and some of Almanzo's walking canes. The Springfield newspaper described her as "a striking, charming little woman. Her white hair was piled high, and held in place by a gold comb that matched her large earrings. She wore a beautiful, very dark red velvet dress, at the shoulder of which a friend had pinned a large orchid. It was difficult to believe that she was 84 years old."[7] Wilder was Mansfield's most famous citizen, and the city is still very proud of her.

In 1953, the new editions of the Little House books, with illustrations by Garth Williams, were published; Wilder was very pleased with them. Then, the next year, the American Library Association created the Laura Ingalls Wilder Award

In the photograph above, Laura Ingalls Wilder (center) is shown at the dedication of the Laura Ingalls Wilder branch of the Wright County Library System on September 28, 1951. On the left is Paxton Price, Missouri State Librarian, and on the right is Docia Holland, Wright County Librarian.

to pay tribute to authors who had written long-lasting and important children's books. The award was a bronze medal, and Wilder was the first recipient.

Wilder's sense of adventure and her curiosity continued well into old age. When she was 87, she visited Rose in Danbury, Connecticut, traveling by airplane for the first time. It must have felt like an exciting and strange experience, especially for someone who used to do all of her traveling in a horse-drawn buggy.

Although Wilder lived alone at Rocky Ridge, she seemed to always have visitors. Friends often checked on her, and Rose made many visits from Connecticut. Local children sometimes stopped by, eager to meet their favorite author. Wilder served them milk and cookies, and then she told them the stories that they loved to hear.

At age 89, Wilder's mind remained engaged, but her body inevitably weakened. Still, she felt strong and independent, and she hoped that she would live beyond 90, as Almanzo had. When Rose arrived for Thanksgiving in 1956, she immediately saw that her mother was sick, and she took her to the hospital, where Wilder was diagnosed with diabetes. She stayed in the hospital for many weeks, and on the day after Christmas, she returned to Rocky Ridge.

Three days after her birthday, on February 10, 1957, Wilder passed away. She was 90 years old. There was a great sadness in Mansfield, Missouri, and all over the world, but her work continues to inspire and delight readers. The Little House books have been cherished by many generations, giving children and adults a glimpse into America's frontier past and also telling heartwarming stories about the unforgettable Ingalls family. Although Laura Ingalls Wilder is gone, her books and memories live in the hearts of children all over the world.

CHRONOLOGY

1860   Charles Philip Ingalls and Caroline Quiner are married on February 1.

1865   Mary Amelia Ingalls is born on January 10.

1867   Laura Elizabeth Ingalls is born to Charles Philip and Caroline Quiner Ingalls on February 7 in log cabin near Pepin, Wisconsin.

1869   The Ingalls family leaves Wisconsin and moves to Kansas.

1870   Carrie Ingalls is born on August 3.

1871   The Ingalls family returns to Pepin, Wisconsin.

1874   The Ingalls family moves to Walnut Grove, Minnesota.

1875   Charles Frederic Ingalls is born on November 1.

1876   The Ingalls family leaves Minnesota and moves to Burr Oak, Iowa; Charles Frederic (baby Freddy) dies on August 27.

1877   Grace Pearl Ingalls is born on May 23.

1878   The Ingalls family moves back to Walnut Grove, Minnesota.

1879   Mary loses her eyesight; the Ingalls family leaves Minnesota and moves to De Smet, Dakota Territory.

1882   Laura becomes a schoolteacher.

1885   Laura and Almanzo Wilder are married on August 25; they make their new home on Almanzo's homestead claim in De Smet.

1886   Rose Wilder is born on December 5.

1888   Laura and Almanzo both suffer from diphtheria; Almanzo is partially paralyzed.

1889   Laura gives birth to a son who dies a short time later; the Wilders' house burns down.

1890–1891   The Wilders move to Spring Valley, Minnesota, and then to Westville, Florida, to aid Almanzo's recuperation from diphtheria.

1892   The Wilders return to De Smet, South Dakota.

1894   The Wilders leave De Smet to travel to the Missouri Ozarks; Wilder keeps diary of trip, later published as *On the Way Home*; Wilders make a down payment on 40-acre property, known as Rocky Ridge Farm.

1902   Charles "Pa" Ingalls dies on June 8.

1908   Rose Wilder moves to San Francisco.

1909   Rose Wilder marries Gillette Lane on March 24; marriage ends in divorce less than 10 years later; only known child died as infant.

1912–1920s   Laura Ingalls Wilder serves as a columnist and as Home Editor of the *Missouri Ruralist*.

1915   Wilder travels to San Francisco to visit Rose.

1917   Wilder takes paid position as secretary-treasurer of Mansfield Farm Loan Association, where she works until 1927.

1919   Wilder writes "The Farmer's Wife Says" for June issue of *McCall's*.

1924   Caroline "Ma" Ingalls dies on April 20.

1925   Wilder publishes "My Ozark Kitchen" in January 17 issue of *Country Gentleman*.

1928   Mary Ingalls dies on October 1928.

1932   Harpers & Brothers of New York publishes *Little House in the Big Woods*.

1941   Grace Ingalls Dow, Wilder's sister, dies on November 10.

1946   Carrie Ingalls Swanzey, Wilder's sister, dies on June 2.

1949   Almanzo Wilder dies of heart failure at Rocky Ridge Farm on October 23.

1954   The Laura Ingalls Wilder Award is established; Wilder is presented with first award.

1957   Laura Ingalls Wilder dies of heart failure at Rocky Ridge Farm on February 10, three days after her ninetieth birthday.

1962   *On the Way Home*, with Rose Wilder Lane, is published.

1968   Rose Wilder Lane dies on October 30.

NOTES

Chapter 1

1 "Laura Ingalls Wilder, Frontier Girl." http://webpages.marshall .edu/~irby1/laura/.

Chapter 2

2 Christopher W. Czajka. "Uncle Sam Is Rich Enough to Give Us All a Farm: Homesteaders, the Frontier, and Hopscotching Across America." PBS: Frontier House. http://www.pbs.org/wnet/ frontierhouse/frontierlife/essay1 .html.

Chapter 4

3 Christopher W. Czajka. "The Descent of Civilization: The Extermination of the American Buffalo." PBS: Frontier House.

http://www.pbs.org/wnet/ frontierhouse/frontierlife/essay8 .html.

Chapter 8

4 Anne T. Earton, "Little House in the Big Woods." *New York Times Book Review* (April 24, 1932): p. 9.

Chapter 9

5 John E. Miller, *Becoming Laura Ingalls Wilder: The Woman Behind the Legend.* Columbia: University of Missouri Press, 1998, p. 228.

6. *Wilder: A Biography.* New York: HarperCollins, 1992, p. 211.

7 Miller, p. 225.

WORKS BY LAURA INGALLS WILDER

1932 *Little House in the Big Woods*

1933 *Farmer Boy*

1935 *Little House on the Prairie*

1937 *On the Banks of Plum Creek*

1939 *By the Shores of Silver Lake*

1940 *The Long Winter*

1941 *Little Town on the Prairie*

1943 *These Happy Golden Years*

1962 *On the Way Home* (with Rose Wilder Lane)

1971 *The First Four Years*

1974 *West From Home* (edited by Roger Lea MacBride)

1988 *A Little House Sampler* (edited by William Anderson)

POPULAR BOOKS

BY THE SHORES OF SILVER LAKE

After the Ingalls family experiences many hardships, they must decide what to do next. Mary loses her eyesight, and the grasshopper plague that destroyed their crops has left the family in debt. They decide to go west to the Dakota Territory, where Pa gets a job working for the railroad. Now in her early teens, Laura takes her first train ride: Laura, Ma, Mary, Carrie, and baby sister Grace meet up with Pa at the railroad camp. Laura describes as much as she can to Mary, who relies on Laura to paint pictures with her words. Pa searches for a homestead claim, and eventually, the Ingalls family leaves the camp to settle on their own land.

FARMER BOY

Almanzo Wilder is a nine-year-old farm boy growing up in the 1860s. He lives with Father, Mother, Royal, Eliza Jane, and Alice on a large farm outside of Malone, New York. Almanzo attends school, takes care of the many chores on the farm, goes to town celebrations, and helps cut ice from a river. Most of all, he wants a horse of his own.

LITTLE HOUSE IN THE BIG WOODS

The first book in the *Little House* series, the novel introduces readers to five-year-old Laura Ingalls and her family: Pa, Ma, Mary, and Baby Carrie. They live in a log cabin in the Big Woods of Wisconsin in 1871. The book includes many realistic details, such as how to make maple sugar and cheese, how to make homemade bullets, as well as vivid descriptions of hog butchering and butter churning. The family faces many dangers, including bears and cold winters, but they take comfort in gathering around the fire at night to listen to Pa play his fiddle.

LITTLE HOUSE ON THE PRAIRIE

This time, Laura and her family travel by covered wagon to the prairies of Indian Territory in southern Kansas. They face many dangers, such as wolves and flooded creeks, but after a long journey, they arrive safely in Kansas. The family accidentally settles on land that belongs to the Osage Indians. Wilder includes details about building a cabin, plowing the fields, and hunting for food. The novel depicts many of the realities of life for settlers on the American frontier 130 years ago.

LITTLE TOWN ON THE PRAIRIE

The long, hard winter is over in De Smet, and the Ingalls family is back on the farm. The book begins when Laura takes a sewing job in town. She also attends social events, such as the July Fourth celebration, and she studies to become a teacher so she can earn money to help send Mary to a school for the blind in Iowa. At school, Nellie Oleson is back, and there is trouble with the new teacher, Miss Eliza Wilder. By the end of the book, Laura passes her teacher's examination and is offered a teaching job, and Mary leaves to attend her new school.

ON THE BANKS OF PLUM CREEK

Laura's family moves from Kansas and starts a new life in southern Minnesota. They settle into a dugout house next to Plum Creek, and Pa borrows money to build a frame house. When Laura and Mary go to the Walnut Grove School, Laura encounters Nellie Oleson, a childhood enemy who appears in several of the *Little House* books. The family enjoys living next to Plum Creek, and Pa is hopeful about the wheat crop. Just before harvest, a gigantic cloud of grasshoppers descends, destroying the fields.

THESE HAPPY GOLDEN YEARS

Fifteen-year-old Laura Ingalls teaches at Brewster School, 12 miles from De Smet. Every Friday, Almanzo Wilder arrives at the school to take her back to her parents' home. Meanwhile, Mary attends a school for the blind in Iowa. After her teaching job is over, Laura returns home, where she continues to go to school in De Smet. The friendship with Almanzo turns to romance, and by the end of the book, Laura and Almanzo are married. This is the last book that Wilder wrote.

ALMANZO WILDER

Almanzo first appears as a nine-year-old boy in *Farmer Boy*. As a young man, Wilder appears again in *The Long Winter*, when he and his friend Cap Garland bravely travel miles away in search of wheat for the starving settlers of De Smet. In the last book in the series, *These Happy Golden Years*, Almanzo, whom Laura calls Manly, drives his beautiful horses 12 miles to pick up Laura from her teaching job, so she can come home for the weekends. Laura and Almanzo's close friendship develops into romance; they get married and move to his homestead claim. Almanzo is optimistic even as they face such hardships such as crop failures, debts, diphtheria, and the loss of their home.

CAROLINE INGALLS

Known as Ma in the *Little House* series, Caroline is patient and gentle. She is also hardworking, helping Pa on the farm, taking care of the home, and raising her four daughters. She is a skilled seamstress, gardener, and cook. Wilder often depicts Ma as sitting in the rocking chair by the fire, sewing. Ma supports Charles's journeys, but she would also like the family to have a stable home that is near town. She brings an air of peacefulness and kindness to the Ingalls family's home.

CARRIE INGALLS

In *Little House in the Big Woods*, Carrie is the baby sister of Laura and Mary. She is too young to be included in her big sisters' adventures; however, after Mary's blindness and the family's move to the Dakota Territory, the books focus more on the interaction between Laura and Carrie. They go to school together in *Little Town on the Prairie*, where they again encounter Nellie Oleson, and they also experience trouble with the new teacher, Miss Eliza Wilder.

CHARLES INGALLS

Known in the *Little House* books as Pa, Charles Ingalls is one of Wilder's most memorable characters. He is a restless spirit who leads his family west in search of land and a place they can call home. Optimistic and good-natured, Pa continues to have hope that the family will prosper, even after grasshoppers destroy their wheat crop and they suffer through the long winter. Pa is an outdoorsman and a hard worker: He hunts, plows the fields, builds a home for the family, butchers hogs, and makes his own bullets. Also a skilled carpenter, he takes on various jobs around town. Pa charms and entertains his family by playing his fiddle and telling stories.

LAURA INGALLS

The star of the *Little House* series, Laura is only five years old in the first book, *Little House in the Big Woods*. She is curious and playful, and she loves to listen to her father's stories about the wilderness. She often protects Mary, her older sister; later, Laura "becomes Mary's eyes" when Mary goes blind. Like her father, Laura loves the West and the outdoors. She is a hard worker, both on the farm and at school. As Laura grows up, readers follow her in her journey from childhood to young adulthood. When she is a teenager, she begins to teach in a one-room schoolhouse, and also spends time with the young homesteader, Almanzo Wilder, whom she later marries. Laura has left a long-lasting impression on children and adults for more than 70 years.

MARY INGALLS

Mary is Laura's oldest sister. In *Little House in the Big Woods*, Mary is a good, quiet girl, with beautiful golden hair that Laura wishes she had. She is two years older than Laura, but she is more timid and easily frightened. As a teenager, Mary is struck with scarlet fever and becomes blind. She is very patient and quiet, and she relies on Laura to describe everything she sees. In *Little Town on the Prairie*, Mary attends a school for the blind in Iowa, where she learns many skills, including how to read Braille.

MR. EDWARDS

Mr. Edwards is a well-loved minor character. The Ingalls family first meets Mr. Edwards on the Osage Indian Reservation in *Little House on the Prairie*, where he helps Pa build the family's cabin. Mr. Edwards is a bachelor, who lives a few miles from the Ingalls family. At Christmas, he travels through a harsh storm to bring the girls presents. Mr. Edwards appears again in *By the Shores of Silver Lake* and *The Long Winter*.

MAJOR AWARDS

1932 *Little House in the Big Woods* is selected for the Junior Literary Guild.

1938 *On the Banks of Plum Creek* is named an ALA Newbery Honor Book.

1940 *By the Shores of Silver Lake* is named an ALA Newbery Honor Book.

1941 *The Long Winter* is named an ALA Newbery Honor Book.

1942 *Little Town on the Prairie* is named an ALA Newbery Honor Book.

1944 *These Happy Golden Years* is named an ALA Newbery Honor Book.

1954 The Laura Ingalls Wilder Award is established; Laura Ingalls Wilder is presented with the first award.

BIBLIOGRAPHY

Anderson, William. *Laura Ingalls Wilder: A Biography.* New York: HarperCollins, 1992.

Czajka, Christopher W. "The Descent of Civilization: The Extermination of the American Buffalo," PBS: Frontier House. Available online. URL: http://www.pbs.org/wnet/frontierhouse/frontierlife/essay8.html.

Czajka, Christoper W. "Uncle Sam is Rich Enough to Give Us All a Farm: Homesteaders, the Frontier, and Hopscotching Across America," PBS: Frontier House. Available online. URL: http://www.pbs.org/wnet/frontierhouse/frontierlife/essay1.html.

Earton, Anne T. "Little House in the Big Woods." *New York Times Book Review* (April 24, 1932): p. 9.

Miller, John E. *Becoming Laura Ingalls Wilder: The Woman Behind the Legend.* Columbia, Mo.: University of Missouri Press, 1998.

Wilder, Laura Ingalls. *The First Four Years.* New York: Scholastic, 1971.

———. *Little House in the Big Woods.* New York: HarperCollins, 1994.

———. *Little House on the Prairie.* New York: HarperTrophy, 1994.

———. "1947 Letter." Laura Ingalls Wilder: Frontier Girl. Available online. URL: http://webpages.marshall.edu/~irby1/laura/.

———. *On the Banks of Plum Creek.* New York: Scholastic, 1953.

———. *These Happy Golden Years.* New York: Harper & Row, 1971.

———. *West From Home.* Edited by Roger MacBride. New York: Harper & Row, 1974.

Wilder, Laura Ingalls, and Rose Wilder Lane. *On the Way Home.* New York: Harper & Row, 1962.

FURTHER READING

Anderson, William T. *Laura Ingalls Wilder Country*. New York: HarperPerennial, 1995.

———. *Little House Guidebook*. New York: HarperCollins, 1996.

———. *Pioneer Girl: The Story of Laura Ingalls Wilder*. New York: HarperCollins, 1998.

———. *Prairie Girl: The Life of Laura Ingalls Wilder*. New York: HarperCollins, 2004.

Collins, Carolyn Strom. *Inside Laura's Little House: The Little House on the Prairie Treasury*. New York: HarperCollins, 2000.

Erisman, Fred. *Laura Ingalls Wilder*. Boise, Idaho: Boise State University, 1994.

Giff, Patricia Reilly. *Laura Ingalls Wilder: Growing Up in the Little House*. New York: Puffin, 1987.

Hines, Stephen W. *I Remember Laura: Laura Ingalls Wilder*. Nashville: T. Nelson, 1994.

Lasky, K., and Meribah Knight. *Searching for Laura Ingalls: A Reader's Journey*. Photographs by Christopher G. Knight. New York: Macmillan, 1993.

Wilder, Ingalls Laura. *Dear Laura: Letters From Children to Laura Ingalls Wilder*. New York: HarperCollins, 1996.

———. *Little House in the Ozarks: A Laura Ingalls Wilder Sampler: The Rediscovered Writings*. Edited by Stephen W. Hines. Boston: G.K. Hall, 1982.

———. *A Little House Reader: A Collection of Writings*. Edited by William T. Anderson. New York: HarperCollins, 1998.

Wilder, Laura Ingalls, and Rose Wilder Lane. *A Little House Sampler*. Edited by William T. Anderson. New York: Perennial Library, 1988.

Zochert, Donald. *Laura: The Life of Laura Ingalls Wilder*. Chicago: H. Regnery, 1976.

Web sites

"Little House: Big Adventure," HarperCollins Children's Books
http://www.littlehousebooks.com

Laura Ingalls Wilder, Frontier Girl
http://frodo.marshall.edu/~irby1/laura/frames.html

Laura Ingalls Wilder Historic Home and Museum
http://www.lauraingallswilderhome.com

"Laura Ingalls Wilder Website Index," Herbert Hoover Presidential Library and Museum
http://hoover.archives.gov/LIW/index.html

PICTURE CREDITS

INDEX

Almanzo Wilder Home, 53
apple trees, 71, 73
Athenians, 88
awards, 15, 98, 101, 104, 106

On the Banks of Plum Creek, 39–40, 98
Barry Corner School, 36
Bible recitation contest, 44
Big Woods
   departures from, 23, 37
   life in, 21–23
   location of, 19–20
   return to, 31
birth of Laura Ingalls Wilder, 12, 22
blindness, 45, 54
blizzards, 51–52
bookkeeping job, 47, 49
Bouchie family, 58
Boylston, Helen, 90
buffalo, 48–49
Burr Oak, 43
butcher shop, 43–44
By the Shores of Silver Lake, 50, 101

cabins, building of, 21
Caroline Years series, 13
cars, 89, 94
Case, John, 80
Chaplin, Charlie, 81
Charlotte's Web, 104
Charlotte Years series, 13
church, 38, 44, 51, 73
cities, visit to, 82–83
Civil War, 22

Cole, Marcus, 69
Congregational Church, 51
Cooley family, 68, 73
Crockett, Davy, 25

Dakota Territory, 48
death of Laura Ingalls Wilder, 108
De Smet, South Dakota, 50, 53, 68
diabetes, 108
diphtheria, 63–64, 105
divorce, 88
donkeys, 72, 73
dugout houses, 37–38

education
   love of, 44
   Mary and, 54
   Rose and, 72, 73, 78
   in Walnut Grove, 36, 38–39
Ensign, Howard, 44

fan resources, 91
Farmer Boy, 98
"Farm Home" column, 80
Farm Loan Association, 87–88, 89
"Favors the Small Farm," 80
feminism, 81
fiddle, 24, 35–36
fireplaces, 79
fires, 63, 64
The First Four Years, 65
Florida, move to, 67
Forbes, Hiram and Docia (uncle and aunt), 47
Ford, Henry, 81
Free Land, 102

Garland, Cap, 54
Gem City of the Ozarks, 71
ghost writers, 82
Gilbert, Melissa, 28
Gilbert, Stella, 40, 59
grasshoppers, 40–41, 42
Gray, Zane, 106
Great Dakota Boom, 48
Great Depression, 90, 93
Gustafson, Gustaf, 23, 30

hailstorm, 63
These Happy Golden Years, 57–58, 104
hard winter, 51–52
historical sites, 53
Hitler, Adolf, 90–91
Homestead Act, 23, 64–65
Hoover, Herbert, 82
Hurley, Sadie, 45
Let the Hurricane Roar, 82

immigrants, 70
Indian Removal Act, 25
Indians, 25–30, 48–49
Ingalls, Caroline (mother), 12, 20–21, 68
Ingalls, Carrie (sister), 27, 77, 94
Ingalls, Charles (father), 12, 20–21, 68, 77–78
Ingalls, Eliza (aunt), 21, 37, 42
Ingalls, Freddy (brother), 41, 42
Ingalls, Grace Pearl (sister), 43, 77, 94
Ingalls, Mary (sister)
    birth of, 22
    blindness of, 45
    death of, 94
    description of, 12, 34
    education of, 54
    life of, 77
    music and, 59–60

Ingalls, Peter (uncle), 21, 37, 42
Iowa College for the Blind, 54

Japan, publication in, 103
Jefferson, Thomas, 50
Justice of the Peace, 50

Kansas, 22–25, 31

land claims, 26–27
Land of the Big Red Apple, 68
Landon, Michael, 28
Lane, Gillette, 81, 88
Lane, Rose. *See* Wilder, Rose (daughter)
Laura Ingalls Wilder Award, 106–107
Laura Ingalls Wilder Memorial Society, 53
Let the Hurricane Roar, 82
Libertarian Party, 82
libraries, 88, 106, 107
Little House in the Big Woods
    Carrie and, 27
    content of, 31
    Osage Indians and, 28–29
    publication of, 94–95
    writing of, 14, 93–94
Little House on the Prairie
    Carrie and, 27
    content of, 24
    Osage Indians and, 28–29
    publication of, 98
Little Town on the Prairie, 101–102
The Long Winter, 101, 103
Louisiana Purchase, 23

MacArthur, Douglas, 103
MacBride, Roger, 13, 82
malaria, 30
manifest destiny, 25
Mansfield, Missouri, 71, 87–88
Martha Years series, 13

Masters, Genevieve, 40, 44, 54
Masters, George and Maggie, 44–45, 52
Masters Hotel, 53
Mein Kampf, 90–91
merchandise, 16
miniseries, 69
Minnesota, move to, 37
Missouri Ruralist, 80
molasses, snow and, 36–37
money
    debt and, 47, 61–63, 74
    grasshoppers and, 40–41, 42
    royalties and, 101
mortgages, 63
movies, 69
museums, 53

Native Americans, 25–30, 48–49
Nebraska, 69
Newberry Honor awards, 15, 98, 101, 104
"New Woman," 81
nicknames, 59

Oconomowoc River, 20–21
Old Home Town, 82, 99
Oleson, Nellie, basis for character of, 40, 44
Osage Diminished Reserve, 25, 98
Osage Indians, 25–30
Owens, Nellie, 39–40, 44
Owens, Willie, 39–40
Ozark Mountains, 68, 70

Panama Canal, 83
paralysis, Alamanzo and, 64
Pearl Harbor, 104
Pepin, Wisconsin, 20, 53
Perry School, 59–60
Pioneer Girl, 92
pioneer life, 34–35, 58, 65

Plum Creek, 37–42
poultry, 80
prairies, 24, 30
prairie schooners, 24
Prohibition, 90
publications, 91

quilting bees, 66
Quiner, Caroline Lake (mother). *See* Ingalls, Caroline
Quiner, Henry (uncle), 21
Quiner, Polly (aunt), 21

railroads, 30, 46, 48
reading, 36, 50, 73, 78
Rock House, 89–90
Rocky Ridge Farm
    building of, 71–72
    love of, 99–100
    sale of, 104–105
    success of, 79–80
Rose Years series, 13
royalties, 101
Russian Hill, 83
Ryland, Cynthia, 13

San Francisco and, 83–85
scarlet fever, 45
schools
    love of, 44
    Mary and, 54
    Rose and, 72, 73, 78
    in Walnut Grove, 36, 38–39
Seal, Silas and Neta, 101
Sewell, Helen, 94
sewing, 54
Shiloh, Battle of, 22
By the Shores of Silver Lake, 50, 101
Shorter, Harland and Gireda, 105
Silver Lake railroad camp, 49
spinoff books, 13, 16
Starr, Mrs., 43

Steadman family, 42
stereotypes, portrayal of Native
  Americans and, 29

teaching, 21, 57–60
television, 16, 28, 69
Trail of Tears, 25

Union Congregational Church, 38

Ven Owen, Professor, 59

wagons, 23–24
Walnut Grove, Minnesota, 37–39,
  43–44
On the Way Home, 68
web sites, 91
West From Home, 83
wheat crops, 40–41, 63
Wilder, Almanzo (husband)
  courtship by, 58–59
  death of, 105
  health of, 63–64, 74
  life with, 60–61
  marriage to, 14, 60
  trip of for food, 54

writing story of, 97–98
Wilder, Eliza, 54
Wilder, Rose (daughter)
  birth of, 14, 63
  education of, 78–79
  as journalist, 81
  naming of, 61
  Rocky Ridge Farm and, 70–71
  San Francisco and, 83–85
  school and, 72, 73
  writings of, 82, 88–90, 102
  writing with, 92–94, 98–99
Wilder Pageant, 53
Wiley, Melissa, 13
Wilkens School, 60
Wilkes, Maria D., 13
Wilkins, Celia, 13
Williams, Garth, 104, 106
Wilson, Woodrow, 87
winters, 36, 40, 51–52
World's Fair, 83–85
World War I, 87
World War II, 103–104
writing, beginnings of, 80–81

Young Pioneers, 82

ABOUT THE CONTRIBUTOR

AMY SICKELS is a fiction writer who lives in Brooklyn, New York. She teaches creative writing classes at Gotham Writers' Workshop. Her short stories and essays have been published in a variety of literary journals.